WHY
Grace
Changes
EVERYTHING

CHUCK SMITH

HARVEST HOUSE PUBLISHERS
Eugene, Oregon 97402

Unless otherwise indicated, all Scripture quotations in this book are taken from the King James Version of the Bible.

Verses marked NKJV are taken from the New King James Version, Copyright © 1979, 1980, 1982 by Thomas Nelson, Inc., Publishers. Used by permission.

Verses marked NIV are taken from the Holy Bible, New International Version®. Copyright © 1973, 1978, 1984 by the International Bible Society. Used by permission of Zondervan Publishing House. The "NIV" and "New International Version" trademarks are registered in the United States Patent and Trademark Office by International Bible Society.

Cover photography © by Adamsmith/Westlight

Edited by Steve Halliday

WHY GRACE CHANGES EVERYTHING

Copyright © 1994 by Harvest House Publishers
Eugene, Oregon 97402

Library of Congress Cataloging-in-Publication Data

Smith, Chuck, 1927 June 25–
        Why grace changes everything / Chuck Smith.
        p.   cm.
        ISBN 1-56507-227-8 (Cloth)
        ISBN 1-56507-373-8 (Trade Paper)
        1. Grace (Theology).   I. Title.
        BT761.2.S65   1994   94-10725
        234—dc20   CIP

Printed in the United States of America.

95   96   97   98   99   00   —   10   9   8   7   6   5   4   3   2

To my precious wife, Kay,
whose faithfulness and love
are a constant inspiration

Contents

A Love Relationship with God

Have you ever pondered the significance of the simple phrase, "God loves you"? It may embody the most important truth anyone can grasp: that God has called us into a loving relationship with Himself. Our part is simply to trust and believe in the deep care and compassion God freely extends to us.

How beautiful it is to experience the freedom and joy of a love relationship with God! Yet how sad it is that there are so many who insist on relating to God in a legalistic way. Their righteousness is based on what they can do for the Lord instead of on what He has already done for them. They carry around a huge list of "do's and don'ts" to keep them bound to God.

I am no stranger to that depressing kind of negative righteousness. As I was growing up, I considered myself one of the most godly kids on the block because of what I *didn't* do. I didn't smoke. I didn't dance. I didn't go to shows. I was taught that such things were utterly sinful. So not only did I avoid those things, I also believed I was far more righteous than my weaker friends who indulged in them. I thought I was much more holy than the preacher's kid, who was known to pick up old cigarette butts and smoke them on the sly. I was above all that, and I was sure God noticed.

Still, I had a big problem. Although I didn't go to shows, I longed to see *Snow White*, so I felt condemned. I would get saved again every Sunday night and would promise God that next week was

going to be different. I was lucky if my relationship
with Him made it past breakfast Monday morning.

Because my righteousness was a matter of
willpower and effort, before long my relationship
with God became a tremendous strain. Every
summer I would attend our church youth camp. On
the last evening we would build a huge bonfire and
gather around to sing worship choruses such as "I
Surrender All" and "I Will Follow Thee, My Lord."
During this emotionally charged time we were asked
to write out on paper either an area of our lives that
we wanted God to change or a commitment we
wanted to make. Each of us would then take a pine
cone, wedge our commitment paper into it, and toss
it in the fire. As I watched my pine cone burn, tears
would run down my cheeks. I would tell God that I
wanted my life to be consumed by His love and that I
wanted to give myself completely over to serving
Him.

As we left the bonfire we were directed to a little
table where camp leaders had laid out a stack of cards
that read, "I promise, by the grace of God, that in the
coming year I will never enter a theater, I will never
smoke a cigarette, I will never drink an alcoholic
beverage, I will never use foul language, and I will
not attend any dances." We would sign these commitment cards and carry them around with us in our
wallets all year long.

I was careful to keep all my commitments—but I
also ended up in a draining, legalistic relationship
with God. I had very little joy in my walk with Christ
because I was tied to God by a contract. I couldn't
break my agreement; hadn't I signed and dated it,
and didn't I carry it around with me in my back
pocket? No, I was committed to keeping this agreement and I fiercely believed that God owed me something for my efforts. God *had* to be good to me . . . at

least, better to me than He was to those who didn't follow through on their commitments.

Imagine my shock, then, when my friends who weren't nearly as righteous as I won the contest where we tried to guess the number of jelly beans in the jar! I would grow angry and ask, "God, why didn't You bless me? You *know* I deserve to win more than they do." The more I thought about it, the more confused I became. Here I was keeping my end of the bargain, yet God seemed to pay no attention at all. I constantly felt let down.

Every once in a while, of course, I would get honest with myself and begin to see that I wasn't nearly as righteous as I liked to think. I knew that my attitude frequently was not what it should have been. There were moments when I knew I had thoroughly fallen short of God's will for my life. I recall a time in high school when I snuck into a show. For six months afterwards I lived in utter condemnation because I had broken my commitment. Often I would give up on the idea that God would ever see fit to bless me. There were a lot of things I wanted to pray for, but what right did I have to ask Him for anything when I had failed Him so miserably?

This heavy burden of works-righteousness carried over into my early ministry years in Tucson, Arizona. It didn't take long for me to realize that there had to be more to ministry than what I was experiencing, more to a relationship with God than what I enjoyed. To make matters worse, I would watch the meetings of some of the major evangelists of the day as they passed through the state, and see tents jammed with people being saved and others experiencing what seemed to be miraculous healings.

I longed to see that kind of power evident in my own life and ministry. Therefore I began earnestly to seek God with fasting and prayer out in the Tucson desert. I would take off alone to wait on the Lord with only a jug of water, a Bible, and a notebook for company. I begged God for His blessing, His power, and His anointing on my life. After a round of such spiritual discipline, I would work up a sense of excitement, believing that God was about to bless our church because I had fasted and prayed. I could hardly wait for the next service to see what God was going to do.

Unfortunately, I grew so weak from fasting that by Sunday I could hardly stand up behind the pulpit. My mind would wander so much that I could barely present a coherent message. The people would fall asleep and I would feel devastated. Here I had expected a tremendous move of God . . . and instead, a chorus of snoring broke out. I would get frustrated and angry and think, *But God, haven't You seen how I have fasted and prayed? Surely You ought to bless this church—and me too, while You're at it!*

I did not understand at the time that my fasting and praying were attempts to obligate God, to force Him to do what I wanted. I thought if people could just see miracles like those described in the book of Acts, they would be convinced about the reality of Jesus Christ.

But later I discovered that the ultimate witness we can offer the world is the love we have for one another, a love that flows from the very heart of God Himself. Conforming to rules and regulations simply can't produce that kind of love relationship. We can try to impose the law on our relationships, but God's love is the only way to gain the stability and security we long for. The Bible tells us that love is the fulfillment of the law. In fact, when asked which was the greatest commandment, Jesus replied that it was to love the Lord with all our heart, mind, soul, and strength, and to love our neighbor as

ourself. Love, not the law, is the key to our relationship with God and with one another.

God wants us to experience the beauty of being
drawn to Him by a cord far stronger than the
obligation and guilt of the law. If we were still
bound to God by a list of rules and regulations, we
would soon find ourselves chomping at the bit and
struggling against the restraints. There is a huge
difference between being bound in relationship by the
joy of love, and being tied up in obligation and guilt.

God never intended that His people be bound by
an endless list of external pressures. It isn't pleasing
to God to hear us moan and complain, "What a drag!
I have to go to church again when there are a
hundred other things I'd rather do. But if I don't
go, God won't love me anymore and the preacher will
give me the evil eye for missing his sermon."

If we find ourselves laboring under such
burdensome attitudes, it is a sure indicator that we
are not operating in a love relationship with God,
but have instead fallen into legalism. God certainly
wants better things for us than a drab, loveless
existence!

God never made out a long contract that says,
"Abide by all my terms and I will love you and bless
you; but if you violate even the smallest provision, it's
all null and void and you are out of My kingdom!"
Christians are not bound by any heavy contract to
God. Paul declared that the only thing that con-
strained him was the love of Jesus Christ (2 Corinthians 5:14).

It took years of God's patient work in my life
before I was able to break free of the bondage of self-
righteousness. For years I had heard of others getting
a tremendous blessing out of the book of Romans.
Since I was always looking for a blessing, I finally
decided to dig into it. And yet, try as I might, it was

difficult for me to relate to. I decided to persevere anyway and see if I could discover what it was that others found so compelling.

One day as I studied this great book, God did nothing less than revolutionize my relationship with Him. It was there that He revealed to me the meaning of that simple, well-worn, but rarely understood word: *grace*. From that time onward I encountered such a free and loving relationship with God that I could not have cared less if I ever saw a spectacular miracle in my ministry. I discovered that even though I was prone to stumble and fall, my mistakes didn't alienate me from God. My relationship with Christ became less a roller coaster of highs and lows and more of a steady ride in His wonderful love.

Imagine how I felt when I discovered the profound truth, "If God is for us, who can be against us?" (Romans 8:31). For years I had labored under the misconception that God was against me. I pictured Him waiting for me to step out of line so He could send fiery judgment crashing down on me. I finally understood that God wanted me to enjoy the peace of His unconditional love, not the fear that always accompanies legalism. I began to relate to God in a whole new way.

I learned that the law was intended to serve as a protective guide to God's people. Its restraints were to function like a parent's safety guidelines, intended only for the welfare of a child. Once we discover the wonder of God's grace, we need no longer be locked in by the law. We can approach life freely because we love God and won't want to do anything to harm the loving relationship we have with Him. When we know the joy of fellowship with God, we won't want any barriers, any blocks, to come between us.

In fact, the more we experience of God's love, the more He Himself becomes the primary desire and focus of our life. The coercive aspects of the law become unnecessary. We find ourselves longing to please God simply because we love Him.

And that is the greatest joy in life—to experience a genuine love relationship with God. To know that He is for us, that He loves us, is the greatest source of security any person will ever know. Discovering the glorious grace of God was one of the most important events in my whole spiritual experience. I learned to relate to God on an entirely new basis: not on the basis of my works, or of my righteousness, but on the basis of God's love for me through Jesus Christ.

That is grace, and that is what makes life worth living. In fact, it is what makes life—*real* life, *abundant* life, *fulfilling* and *satisfying* life—possible at all. For when our eyes are opened to the astonishing truth that our relationship with God does not depend upon the puny pebble of our own efforts but upon the massive rock of His unchanging and loving character, life opens before us in a technicolor explosion of awesome possibilities.

Grace transforms desolate and bleak plains into rich, green pastures. It changes grit-your-teeth duty into loving, enthusiastic service. It exchanges the tears and guilt of our own failed efforts for the eternal thrill and laughter of freely offered pleasures at the right hand of God. *Grace changes everything!*

Have you discovered the deep joy of living in God's grace? Would you welcome a reminder that our standing with God depends not on our own weak efforts but on what His almighty arm has accomplished for us? Wherever you are in your spiritual journey, I invite you now to take a few moments to consider with me the amazing grace of God poured out on our behalf.

For it's true, you know: *Grace changes everything!*

1
Grace
Forgiven!

ONE EVENING I HEARD a speech by former Secretary of State Dr. Henry Kissinger. He told the gathering that his first mistake is mentioned in his autobiography on page 1159. He also noted it was his last mistake.

If I were to write an autobiography, my first mistake would probably be found in the prologue to the book, if not in the table of contents itself! There is no way I would ever try to stand before God on the basis of my own goodness. It's not that I am some rotten, morally depraved individual; it's just that I am nowhere near good enough to be acceptable before an absolutely holy God.

A Dead-End Righteousness

One very common way of trying to become righteous is to define what righteousness is and isn't, to set up a code, and then live according to this code. There's only one problem: No one ever lives up to their own code, so we conjure up a great number of excuses to explain why we fail. The most common is that our failure isn't really our fault.

If I drop a glass and break it, it isn't that I am uncoordinated; it's because someone called me when he shouldn't have. Others were making too much noise in the other room, so my mistake is really their fault. "Look what you caused me to do!" I say. "You made me do it, so it isn't my fault." None of us like to accept blame.

This attitude goes all the way back to Adam. He blamed his failure on Eve. "The woman that you gave to be my wife," he told God, "it's *her* fault that I am the way I am" (*see* Genesis 3:12). Proverbs declares, "There is a generation that are pure in their own eyes, and yet is not washed from their filthiness" (Proverbs 30:12).

If you think you are a very pure person and yet are not washed from your filthiness, righteousness has evaded you. The Bible says, "If we say that we have no sin, we deceive ourselves, and the truth is not in us. . . . If we say that we have not sinned, we make Him a liar, and His word is not in us" (1 John 1:8,10). Scripture states our problem clearly: "All the world [stands] guilty before God. . . . all have sinned and come short of the glory of God" (Romans 3:19,23).

Whenever we try to establish our righteousness by keeping rules, eventually we are forced to admit we operate on a sliding scale. I will always look morally better to myself than I do to you, and you will always look morally worse to me than you do to yourself. I can look at your life and see all kinds of flaws; but when I look at myself, the few flaws I notice don't seem so bad.

Even the righteousness I *can* achieve by what I do is only a sham righteousness. The Bible declares, "We are all as an unclean thing, and all our righteousnesses are as filthy rags" (Isaiah 64:6).

If our relationship with God depended upon being righteous and good, we would never make it.

It's almost comical to see some people parade around in their rags. They saunter around with their "holier than thou," gaudy kind of religiosity, with a hyperspiritual air about them. They talk in whispered tones because they think it sounds holy and righteous. They use King James English because, as we all know, "Thees" and "Thous" are far more righteous than "yous" and "yours." We see them puffed out in their righteousness, strutting around, showing off...and God shakes His head and says, "Filthy rags."

If my relationship with God depended upon my being righteous and good, I would never make it. I have failed. I have come short of the glory of God. The best that I can manage is when I am having a good day, my biorhythms are right, and everything is going well—really flowing. I'm cool. Man, I am really something. But even on my best days God looks down and says, "Filthy rags." My best efforts simply aren't enough.

Trying to keep the law condemns me, for the true law deals with inward attitudes. Back when I labored under this standard of self-righteousness, I found I resented certain things other people were doing. I became bitter. I realized that I hated certain people and that I was jealous and covetous of the things they owned. I noticed I had violated my own code and had wiped out my relationship with God. Nothing was left to do but to start all over again.

Unfortunately, just about the time I would feel as though I were restoring a right relationship with God, something happened. I blew up and down I went again. I would be forced to start climbing the ladder of good works once more until I got to the rung where I finally felt I could relate to God. No sooner would I reach that rung, however, than somebody would pull a stupid move on the freeway and I would yell, "Where did you get your driver's license, you idiot?" And the whole process would start all over again.

What's the Standard?

Those who believe that they can be made acceptable to God without Jesus need to deal with some crucial questions. If they believe they can make it to heaven by achieving a certain level of goodness, what standard do they have to live up to? What will God require of them? So many say, "I feel that I am basically a kind and good person and am willing to stand before God on my own merit."

But these people fail to take into account that God's standards are different than ours. Jesus showed us God's requirement for those who would strive for heaven on their own power when He said, "Be ye therefore perfect, even as your Father which is in heaven is perfect" (Matthew 5:48). The standard for

the person who wants to be right with God is nothing
short of absolute perfection—not just trying hard, or
being sincere, but a flawless keeping of all God
ever intended for man. Clearly, those who believe
they can earn eternal life by their good works have a
distorted understanding of the holiness of God and
what it means to be right with God.

If we are going to set up a standard of righteous
conduct, we need to use the one established by Jesus
Christ. Jesus is the only person whose life prompted
God to say, "This is my beloved Son, in whom I am
well pleased" (Matthew 3:17). To enjoy fellowship
with God, we must be as righteous as Jesus. In John
16:8,10 Jesus said, "And when he [that is, the Holy
Spirit] is come, he will reprove the world of . . .
righteousness, because I go to my Father, and ye see
me no more." Jesus' ascension into heaven was God's
witness to the world about His Son. It is as if He
were saying, "*This* is the righteousness that I will
accept in heaven." Jesus' life is the only standard of
righteousness. If I want to be accepted by God, I
must be as righteous as Jesus Christ. The Scriptures
show that there is only one kind of righteousness that
God will accept: the very righteousness of Christ
Himself. So, if we want to stand before God on the
basis of our own good works, we must live a life that
measures up to the goodness we see in Jesus.

But I realize that is impossible. I can't achieve
that kind of righteousness. Jesus Himself said, "I say
unto you, That whosoever looketh on a woman to lust
after her hath committed adultery with her already in
his heart" (Matthew 5:28). He said, "I say unto you,
That whosoever is angry with his brother without
a cause shall be in danger of the judgment" (Matthew
5:22). He further said, "Love your enemies, do good
to them which hate you. Bless them that curse you,
and pray for them which despitefully use you. And

unto him that smiteth thee on the one cheek offer also the other; and him that taketh away thy cloak forbid not to take thy coat also. Give to every man that asketh of thee; and of him that taketh away thy goods ask them not again" (Luke 6:27-30). And He commanded us to "love ye your enemies, and do good, and lend, hoping for nothing again" (Luke 6:35).

How can anybody be *that* righteous? I know I can't. I've failed miserably. Does that mean, then, that I must forever be alienated from God? Is there no way I can ever enjoy fellowship with God? Do I have to go on in this emptiness, in this frustration, seeking after and reaching out for something I can never obtain?

If there is any hope for us to be forgiven by God, there must be another basis for it other than our works. As Paul declares, "By the deeds of the law there shall no flesh be justified in his sight" (Romans 3:20).

If we are ever to enjoy fellowship with God, it will have to be on some basis other than our own righteousness. The rules that God has established for righteousness are far too stringent for us to abide by. We can't do it. Our only hope is that another form of righteousness has been provided for us, a righteousness based on a totally different principle than our own works.

Thank God, there is such a principle! It's called *grace*.

What Is Grace?

The root meaning of the word *grace* is "beauty." In the New Testament, grace means "God's unmerited favor." Grace is God giving to me something that I cannot obtain on my own. Grace is being accepted by God even though I do not deserve it, even though I am not worthy of it.

The Bible teaches that I receive grace on the basis of my belief and trust in God. Hebrews 11:6 declares that without faith it is impossible to please God. We are forgiven by a holy God simply by believing in Jesus Christ and in His death on our behalf. When we place our trust in Him, our slate is wiped clean.

It is not possible for us to be forgiven by complying with any law or religious system. It was necessary that Christ go to the cross in order that He might establish the basis whereby I can approach God.

When Jesus was praying in the garden, He said, "Father, if thou be willing, remove this cup from me: nevertheless not my will, but thine, be done" (Luke 22:42). He was saying, "If it is possible that men can be saved by any other means than My death—if they can be saved by being religious, by somehow gaining their own righteousness—then I do not want to go to the cross. Please don't put Me through this horrible ordeal." But it was not possible, and so He went to the cross, died, was buried, and rose again. His death made it possible for God to extend His grace to you and me.

Perhaps an illustration will help to make this clear. Imagine that you were charged with a crime. You are accused of trespassing on a neighbor's property. As any defense attorney knows, there are two possible ways for you to be cleared of the charge. You may seek to prove that you didn't trespass on his property, or you may seek to prove that you had every right to be there.

Now apply this logic to our spiritual situation. God has charged us with being sinners—for rebelling against His law and His will. He has charged us with unrighteousness.

How can we be justified from those charges?
We can't say that we are innocent, for we are guilty.
All of us have sinned. Nor can we say that we had a
right to do what we did because we had no such
right. Our actions were clearly wrong. How, then,
can the law be of value to us in our desire to be forgiven? The answer is, it can't. The case is open
and shut. We didn't have a right to do it, we did it
anyway, and thus we stand guilty.

The Great Bank Robbery

Let's change the illustration. Suppose that I
robbed a bank willfully and deliberately. The law condemns me because I can't say I didn't do it or prove
that I didn't do it. The video camera caught me. I
can't say I had a right to do it because robbery is not
included in the First Amendment. Therefore, there is
no way I can be forgiven within the law.

During the trial, I might try to say, "I promise I
won't rob any more banks as long as I live. I will live
a good, clean life from now on. I will never take
anything from anybody wrongfully again." That still
doesn't justify me from what I have *already* done. I
might try to say that I should be forgiven because I
did so much good with the money. I gave some to the
church and I fed my family. But my "righteous"
deeds cannot counterbalance or absolve my guilt.

The judge may order that I pay back to the bank
all the money that I took. As part of my sentence, he
may order me to pick up tin cans along the freeway
to help keep America beautiful. I may spend the rest
of my life doing good things, but still I will not be
absolved of what I have done. All the works of the
law cannot erase my guilt. My past wrongdoings still
exist. I am a robber and the verdict is clear.

Why is it, then, that in spiritual matters so many
people seek to plead innocent before God by virtue
of all their good works?

There are many of us who respond to our sin,
guilt, and unrighteousness with regret and new
resolutions. We want to make amends and turn over
a new leaf. But those efforts can't win our forgiveness. Even our best efforts cannot take away the guilt
of what we have already done. We can never be justified by good works. Even a whole life of good
works cannot atone for a single sin.

God's basis of forgiveness is the sacrifice of His
only begotten Son. All of our guilt—all of our past
and future wrongdoings—have been laid to the
charge of Jesus Christ, the innocent Lamb, the perfect
one who knew no sin. He died for us. He bore our
guilt; He suffered and died for our sins. Paul wrote,
"For He hath made him to be sin for us, who knew
no sin; that we might be made the righteousness of
God in him" (2 Corinthians 5:21). Jesus became sin
for us that we might be pardoned through Him. In
other words, He switched places with us. "Though
he was rich, yet for your sakes he became poor, that
ye through his poverty might be rich" (2 Corinthians
8:9). He has taken our sin and forgiven us through
our simple faith and trust in Him.

Jesus, Our Hope

When God laid on Jesus the iniquity of us all,
Christ received the judgment due us for our sins. He
received our deserved punishment, which the Bible
declares is death (*see* Romans 6:23). God has declared
that if we will believe in Jesus Christ as our Lord
and Savior, we will be forgiven of every wrong thing
we have ever done. "The blood of Jesus Christ His
Son cleanses us from all sin," says 1 John 1:7. This

cleansing is something the law could never do; it is a provision of grace.

---

*We can strive to make it
to heaven on our own
efforts or we can place
our faith in Jesus.*

The fact is, faith is our *only* hope. Our good deeds or efforts or works can never earn us forgiveness from God. Paul declared in strong words, "But to him that worketh not, but believeth on Him that justifieth the ungodly, his faith is counted for righteousness" (Romans 4:5). To him who is not working, but simply believing, God imputes righteousness. God gives us this forgiveness because of our faith in the finished work that Jesus Christ has done for us.

The Choice Is Yours

You have a choice. You can strive to make it to heaven by your own efforts and try to be as good as Christ, or you can place your faith in Jesus and receive your right standing with God as a gift of His grace.

For me, this is no choice at all. I know there is no way that I, in my good works, would ever make it to heaven. I stand hopelessly condemned on the basis of my past sin. I have no chance of being received by God apart from His mercy.

The good news is, God has provided a way of acceptance before Him. God, who is absolutely holy and pure and so righteous that no sin can dwell in

His presence, has made a way for people like us to have fellowship with Him. When we believe in this sacrifice that Jesus Christ made for us—even though we didn't deserve it—the Father grants us perfect forgiveness.

That's the gospel of grace. Each one of us can relate to God, even though we are far from perfect. We can still have a beautiful relationship with God through His Son Jesus Christ.

When we relate to the Father by faith through His Son, we have a solid relationship. We are now sons of God. Because He is our Father, we don't have to wonder if we are worthy to come to Him. We do not come on the basis of our worthiness, but on the basis of our relationship with Him.

That is what the gospel of grace is all about. God looks at us as though we never committed a single trespass against Him. Now, I have trouble looking at myself like that. I look at myself in the mirror and say, "Chuck, you are a sinner. You can't control your appetite; you have so many flaws." And yet God looks at me and says, "Forgiven." He loves me and accepts me as I am because I am in Jesus Christ. Even as He has accepted His own Son, so now He accepts me. Paul tells us that we have been accepted "in the beloved" (Ephesians 1:6). The Beloved one is Christ; and you, being in Christ, are accepted by God just as Christ is accepted.

That is why the gospel of grace is the best news I have ever heard. God forgives us because we believe in His Son, whom He sent to die for our sins. All our sins have been blotted out. There is no accounting of guilt. As Paul tells us, "Oh, how happy are they whose iniquities are forgiven, and whose sins are covered. Oh, how happy is the man to whom the Lord does not impute sin" (*see* Romans 4:7,8).

As sons of God, we have every right to come to our Father to ask Him for anything that we might need. We have every right to trust the wisdom of our Father to either grant or deny the request, according to His knowledge of what is best for us. We can commit ourselves to our heavenly Father, who loves us so very much. He will give us only what is best.

What a joy it is to know that God desires to bestow upon us the richness and the fullness of His love—not because we deserve it, but because He loves us. This is the gospel of grace in Jesus Christ!

2
Grace

The Door Is
Never Closed

A S WONDERFUL AS IT is, forgiveness is only half the story of the gospel of grace. There are many people who believe God has forgiven us in Christ. Where they have trouble is the second half of the good news: That just by believing in Jesus Christ, God accounts us righteous.

Not everybody believes that—not by a long shot. Various groups have established standards of righteousness, yet they seldom agree upon what those standards should be.

Is Gold In or Out?

Not so very long ago, some groups taught that it was unrighteous to wear buttons. They used hooks and eyes for their garments and wouldn't think of wearing buttons on anything. "You wear buttons?" they'd say. "How unrighteous can you be? Shame!" Even today there are groups who teach that wearing gold is utterly sinful; you cannot possibly be righteous if you wear gold. Throughout history people have established varying standards of righteousness—always with the idea that if they adhered to this particular standard, God would accept them.

There is, however, a real problem with trying to establish a righteousness by laws or by works. The fact is, we rarely live up even to our own standards!

Each of us accepts a moral standard that we consider good and right. This is what I really am, or at least what I would be were it not for outside hindrances. Psychologists call it our "superego," our ideal self. Unfortunately, no one knows the "real me." Why? Because the "real me" is perfect. In fact, I don't even know the real me because circumstances constantly keep me from being as wonderful as I really am.

Along with the superego, psychologists talk about the "ego," which is the real self, the true you. Sadly, the true you is never up to the standards of the ideal you.

Now, if there is a vast difference between your superego and your ego, you're considered a maladjusted person. On the other hand, if you know you're not perfect and you don't have such a high standard for the ideal you, then you are congratulated as a well-adjusted person.

Psychologists often seek to bring down the standards of a person's superego by telling the patient he has set impractical goals. "Nobody is that perfect; nobody is that good," they will say. "What you are doing isn't so abnormal. Everybody does it. You shouldn't be trying to set such high standards for yourself!" These therapists are constantly trying to narrow the difference between the superego and the ego so that we might enjoy more well-balanced lives. They seek a cure by bringing down the superego.

Contrast that with the work of Jesus. He doesn't try to lower the superego; He aims to bring up the ego. He wants to lift up the real you!

Even though the real me is well below the ideal me, nevertheless I am righteous before God and He looks at me as perfectly righteous because of my faith in Jesus Christ.

This is the second aspect of the gospel of grace. First, all of your sins have been taken care of, washed, and forgiven because of your faith in Jesus Christ. Second, God looks at you as righteous because of your believing in Jesus Christ. Apart from what you are doing or not doing, apart from keeping any code of ethics, God is imputing righteousness to your account because you believe upon Jesus Christ.

This is the glorious gospel, the good news. To know that God accepts me by my faith in Jesus Christ and that my righteousness is through faith in Jesus Christ is good news indeed!

The Door Is Open

Why is it such good news? I never need to fear and say, "Oh, I dare not go to God, because I just told a lie. I just lost my temper. I just deceived that person. Oh, I have no right to ask God to help me now because I failed in that task." If my righteousness comes by my works, then Satan can bar the door to God practically all the time, because I am never doing as much as I feel I should. I am never as good as I know I ought to be. I haven't achieved my superego. I haven't lived up to my own standards of what I feel is right. Because I have failed to achieve those

ideal standards, Satan will use my failure to keep me
from coming to God. "You have no right to ask
God to help you when you have just failed Him
again. You know your action is displeasing to God,
yet you did it anyhow. Now you're in trouble and
now you want God to help you. You think He is
going to listen to you? No way!"

Satan can always bar the door to God if he can
cause me to look within myself and at myself. But if I
am looking to Jesus Christ and I realize that I am
accounted righteous because of my faith in Christ,
Satan can never bar the door.

Oh, he still comes to me and says, "Chuck, you
are a rotten wretch. You have no right to stand up in
front of people and proclaim the glorious good news
of Jesus Christ. You have no right to stand up there
and teach the Word of God. You have failed in this
area and you have failed in that area. You are a
mess!"

I always start to smile whenever this happens,
because I'm sure I have gotten by with a few things—
I know there are a few things he hasn't even brought
up! I say to him, "Satan, you don't scare me with
your accusations; you are not going to cause me to
run off and hide someplace. In fact, I know that what
you say is true. I know that I have failed. I know that
I have a weakness. But you don't drive me *from* Jesus
Christ; you are driving me *to* Him, because my only
hope is the cross of Jesus Christ!"

And so I flee to the only place where I am safe,
the only place where I have any hope at all. Surely I
have no hope in my own self and in my own righteousness. But I have great hope in the work that
Jesus Christ did for me and in the work God is doing
in me by the power of His Holy Spirit as He is conforming me into the image of Christ.

Those things that I cannot do for myself, He is doing for me. Those areas where I was so weak, He has made me strong. I have recognized my weakness and I have cast myself helplessly upon Him. In those areas where I was once weak and constantly stumbling, now I stand strong because His strength has been made perfect in my weakness (*see* 2 Corinthians 12:9).

Certainly, I am not yet all that God wants me to be. Far from it! But thank God, I am not what I was. Even in my present state of imperfection, God looks upon me and accounts me righteous and holy. That is why I never want to be caught anywhere except in Christ Jesus. We must never see ourselves apart from Him.

No Degrees of Righteousness

If God has imputed the righteousness of Christ to us because we have believed, then it is folly for us to try to improve on that righteousness by doing works. We can't improve on God's righteousness. There is no way we can improve on the right standing that He has imputed to us. We *are* righteous. That is God's accounting of our life because we believe and trust in the work of Jesus Christ.

*Our righteousness now
and for eternity is a result
of our simple faith in
God's Son, Jesus.*

No one in heaven will be boasting about how righteous they made themselves. We will not have to listen to Abraham or David or Paul go on and on about all the wonderful things they did to achieve a righteous standing before God. These men simply believed God, and their faith was accounted to them for righteousness.

None of us will stand in heaven comparing good works with one another because there will only be one who will receive glory before the throne of God. There will be only one shining star. There won't be some kind of spiritual caste system where some will bask in the glory of their works while others of us will stand in the corner wondering how we made it there at all. Jesus and Jesus alone will receive the glory for our salvation. If it were not for Him, none of us would be there.

As Paul put it, "God forbid that I should glory, save in the cross of our Lord Jesus Christ" (Galatians 6:14). No matter how many good deeds we've done for Him, no matter how many people we lead to Him or how many churches we establish for Him, our only glory is in Jesus Christ, who died for us. Our righteousness is not a question of good works, human efforts, or in keeping certain rituals or dietary laws. Our righteousness—both here and now and for all eternity—is a result of our simple faith in God's Son, Jesus.

Righteousness by faith removes all distinctions between those who belong to Christ. I am no better than you, or you than me. We are all sinners, saved only by God's glorious grace. There is no other way to right standing before God. There is only one kind of righteousness that God will accept, and that is the imputed righteousness of Jesus Christ.

If I am seeking to relate to God on the basis of my own righteousness or my own works, or if I expect to be blessed because I have been on good behavior this week or I have read so many chapters or prayed so much, then my relationship with God is always going to be tenuous. Sometimes I will feel that my relationship with God is good and at other times I will feel that it is bad. Why? Because I am trying to relate to Him on the basis of my righteousness.

Without grace, my relationship with God is never an established reality and it is impossible to enjoy peace. If my relationship with God were dependent on how I felt or how I was living or on my own righteousness, I would not be able to relate to God most of the time.

When my relationship with God is predicated upon God's grace toward me, however, the door of blessing is never closed. God's blessings are bestowed on the basis of His grace, His unmerited favor. I *never* deserve or earn a blessing. The blessings that come into my life are always predicated upon God's unmerited favor to me. God loves me so much, He blesses me anyway. God is so good! The truest praise is that which rises spontaneously from our hearts as we recognize God's marvelous grace toward us.

A Stubborn Tendency

We find it very difficult to get away from the concept that our righteousness is somehow related to the works we do for God. We tend to consider some believers as more holy than others because of their performance. We can even find ourselves using this standard to judge others. If someone isn't doing the same degree of works or isn't as zealous as we are, then surely this person just isn't as righteous as we are.

It is extremely difficult to remove this idea of righteousness by works from our thinking. Because this notion is so deeply ingrained, many of us face a constant struggle with guilt feelings. Even as Christians we can find ourselves getting set up for damaging guilt episodes. Because we love God we want to adopt personal standards of conduct in keeping with our identity as children of God. Now that Christ dwells within me, I want to manifest His love, which is patient, long-suffering, kind, gentle, and merciful.

And yet how fragile that love in my life can be! I can be driving along on the freeway when a driver in front of me makes a stupid move and endangers my life. Instantly, feelings of anger come rushing into my mind. I want to lay on my horn and ride his bumper and show that idiot how I really feel about his driving. But then, after doing all these mean things, I remember that my license plate says, "CALVARY." At that moment, all my old, familiar guilt feelings pour into my heart. Accusing thoughts like, *What a great witness you are!* flood my mind and leave me feeling totally unrighteous. I've blown it again, failing God once more, and I'm left with a sense of total alienation from Him.

---

*Trying to relate to God on
the basis of effort and
works is always a struggle.
We can't know the peace
of God until we experience
the grace of God.*

What's difficult to grasp is that although my behavior is wrong, it has nothing to do with my right standing with God. It is so hard to disassociate the concept of works and law from the idea of righteousness! My conduct and my standing before God seem to be inseparably related, and yet they are totally unrelated.

The truth is that God Himself has imputed right standing to me simply because I believe in His Son, Jesus Christ. If keeping a list of rules such as "never get angry when driving" or "never lose your temper with your children" could have brought us into a right relationship with God, then my conduct and my standing with God would be related. But there are no rules that give life, because sin has brought alienation and death. In order for us to have life, God had to establish a New Covenant based on better promises than works-righteousness. That New Covenant is the gospel of grace.

Grace and Peace

Maybe you have been a wretch. You have been irritable and miserable and you feel that God can't possibly love you. You feel utterly disgusted with the failure of your flesh. You know that all you deserve is the back side of God's hand in judgment.

Then suddenly, out of the blue, God gives you some glorious blessing. At that moment there rises from your heart spontaneous praise to God in worship. This is the truest form of praise—the kind of worship which erupts spontaneously in response to God's grace. This is the kind of praise that says, "God is so very good to me. I don't deserve a bit of it."

Because I relate to God on the basis of grace I am never, ever, cut off from His blessings. On the other hand, if I am expecting God's intervention on my behalf on the basis of my goodness or my deeds, I am cut off much of the time.

I have discovered that the lack of God's blessings on my life has nothing to do with my outward performance, but rather stems from my lack of faith in God's grace. I have learned that God's blessing is unconditional. The more I see His blessing in my life, the more I realize how totally undeserving I am. Because of this truth, I can have glorious peace. I have no need to worry.

If we are trusting in our righteousness as the basis for our relationship with God, we will never experience consistent peace. Trying to relate to God on the basis of effort and works is always a struggle, always a strain, always pressured. If we are ever to come to know the peace of God, we must realize that this amazing grace of God first flows toward us even though we're rotten and undeserving of it.

Then, after accepting this glorious grace of God, the peace of God fills our hearts and lives. We know that He loves us—even though we are far from perfect, even though we have failed. Even when it seems as if nobody else loves us (and we don't blame them, because we don't even love ourselves), still God loves us.

Have you ever heard of the Siamese twins of the New Testament? They're the two little words, "grace and peace." They are always coupled together, in that order. We might say that the elder of the twins is grace. It is always grace and peace; we never read a salutation of peace and grace. Why? Because that would be putting the cart before the horse. The proper order is *always* grace and peace, because we cannot know the peace of God in our own hearts until we have first experienced the grace of God in our lives.

As Pure as Jesus

The Bible says that someone who places his faith
in Jesus has been "justified." What does that mean?
It means that God has granted us a standing before
Him just as if we had never sinned.

This was no small feat for God to accomplish! For
if we have all sinned and missed the mark, how can
God look at us as if we had never sinned and still be
just? If He sees our lives as they truly are and must
act according to His attribute of justice, how can He
treat us as though we were perfect?

This is where the power of the gospel comes in.
God made the sinless Jesus to be sin for us. The
Scriptures declare that God laid on the innocent
Christ the iniquities of us all. Jesus literally took my
place and took the punishment that was due me as a
guilty sinner.

This is the glorious gospel of grace. We can have
a standing of righteousness before God far superior to
anything we could achieve under the law. For no
matter how meticulously we try to keep the law, we
always fall short. The righteousness which comes
through faith in Christ, however, is imputed to us
and is complete. There is nothing that can be added
to it. In Christ, I have an absolutely perfect, righteous
standing before God. There are no charges against
me. In His eyes, I am perfect. That doesn't mean that
I am a perfect man—not by a long shot! It means
that Jesus Christ is perfect and I have His righteousness credited to my account because of my faith in
Him.

How I praise God for the knowledge of the grace
of God that He brought to my heart and for the love
relationship that I have with Him! It doesn't alter.
It doesn't change when I am depressed, or wrong, or

angry. It is a flowing relationship that is steady and always present. He loves me when I am sweet and He loves me when I am mean. How good it is to know the grace of God and the gospel according to grace!

3

Grace

No Favorites in
the Kingdom

H AVE YOU NOTICED HOW oftentimes the very people we have classified as impossible to save have been marked by God as the next converts? It's not uncommon at Calvary Chapel for long-lost friends to meet unexpectedly in a hallway, look quizzically at each other, and say in unison, "What are *you* doing here?" Seeing each other in church with a Bible in hand and a smile on their face just wipes them out. Neither thought the other could be saved.

I don't suppose very many people in the early church were praying for Saul's salvation. They were probably saying, "Lord, wipe that guy out. He is going to kill the church. Stop him, Lord!" They were probably hoping God would lower the boom in judgment

But God had another way of stopping him, unlike anything they anticipated. God brought Saul's life to a halt as he was on the road to Damascus and there turned him around 180 degrees. Saul was reborn as Paul and became the greatest proclaimer in history of the gospel of grace.

God is a specialist at taking the unlikeliest of candidates and turning them into trophies of His grace. He is able to make a beautiful change in each of us. He can change our value systems and make us new creatures in Christ. He calls us to be examples of what His grace can do.

No One Too Small

Sometimes we make the mistake of thinking God uses only "special" people—the strong, the intelligent, the beautiful. We don't think He has a place for the rest of us. We are so wrong!

God doesn't have "important" people. God uses ordinary people and works through plain people. That is why Paul wrote, "For you see your calling, brethren, that not many wise according to the flesh, not many mighty, not many noble, are called. But God has chosen the foolish things of the world to put to shame the wise, and God has chosen the weak things of the world to put to shame the things which are mighty" (1 Corinthians 1:26,27).

God loves us ordinary folk and endows us with gifts so that we might fill our place in the body of Christ. Any ability we have is a gift from His hand. Everything we have was given to us. As Paul said in 1 Corinthians 4:7, "What do you have that you did not receive?"

How can I glory in my ministry as though I didn't receive it, as though what I am able to share is something of my genius or brilliance? Anything worthwhile I have came from God. There is no way I can be proud and boastful, as though I were somebody independent of Him. Apart from Him, I am nothing. Apart from Him, I can do nothing.

Men often develop an inflated view of their own importance and greatness and gloat over their place in the work of God. But the truth is, God doesn't need any of us. I'm sorry if that makes you feel unimportant, but it's true. He has chosen to use us, but He doesn't have to. He could just as easily use someone else.

To me, that is thrilling. I haven't been chosen to serve because I am so wonderful. God doesn't choose us because of our greatness or abilities or potential. He chooses us because He decides to choose us. Important, proud people do not like that. They are "above" being chosen . . . so usually they are not. God chooses by His grace. He chose me. He chose you.

Heaven is going to be full of surprises. As we look around, the first surprise will be all the people who we thought would never make it. The next surprise will be those sitting in the front row in the places of honor. We will say, "Who are these people? I never saw them before." "Some of them went to Calvary Chapel," someone will say, "but where is Chuck?" And somewhere way out in the back of the crowd, in the peanut gallery, I will yell, "Here I am! Thank God, through His grace, I made it."

All Are Equal in the Kingdom

Prior to meeting Jesus face to face on the road to Damascus, the apostle Paul spent the majority of his life as a Pharisee. The Pharisees, you remember, were members of the strict, legalistic Jewish sect that so strongly opposed Jesus. You get a flavor for who they were by considering their prayers, a few of which have been preserved for us. Every morning the rabbis prayed, "I thank you, Father, that I was not born a Gentile, a slave, or a woman." No doubt this was a part of Paul's devotional life for many years.

How interesting it is, then, that in Galatians 3:28 the apostle turns all three components of this traditional prayer on their heads. He writes, "There is neither Jew nor Greek, there is neither bond nor free, there is neither male nor female: for ye are all one in Christ Jesus."

Jesus has made equal access to God available to all people. God receives us as His dearly loved children—this is the beauty of the gospel.

Jesus is the great equalizer. His grace refuses to elevate one person over another. We all are one because in Christ, God accepts one sinner just as readily as He accepts another. God places tremendous value on each individual.

This gospel has made a tremendous impact wherever in the world it has gone. Consider women's rights. Prior to the arrival of Christianity in New Guinea, women were considered unworthy to worship God. A woman had only to touch a place of worship to be put to death. Such second-class citizenship created a climate of fear and shame and led to an extremely high suicide rate among women. They had very little to live for and oppression was heavy. Imagine the impact on this culture when the gospel of grace appeared on the scene. Suddenly men and women discovered that in Christ there is no distinction between male and female.

Jesus has made equal access to God available to all people regardless of their demographic group. God does not receive us as justified strangers or distant acquaintances, but as His dearly loved children. John tells us that "as many as received him, to them gave he power to become the sons of God, even to them that believe on his name" (John 1:12). This is the beauty of the gospel.

No matter what we have been like or what wrong we have done, if we will place our faith in Christ, we will be pardoned for all our sins. Even beyond this almost incomprehensible blessing, God also receives us as His sons. That is what Paul meant when he wrote, "For ye are all the children of God by faith in Christ Jesus" (Galatians 3:26). The word "children" in this passage literally means "placed as a son."

God doesn't have any important people. The objects of His grace are not only the strong, or the beautiful, or the intelligent. He calls us ordinary folk to His side and wraps His strong arms around us in a gentle embrace of love. This is the gospel of grace.

Chosen by Grace

Paul saw his whole life as the result of God's gracious choice. As he put it, "It pleased God . . . to reveal his Son in me" (Galatians 1:15,16). That is what God wants to do in every one of our lives. That is what God wants to do in you now. God desires to reveal His Son to the world through you.

In fact, God has been working in your life since the moment you were conceived to make you the perfect instrument to reveal His Son. That is why Paul wrote, "God... separated me from my mother's womb, and called me by his grace" (Galatians 1:15). It is remarkable to see how God prepared Paul for his ministry long before he had one.

God knew He was going to need a special person to bring the gospel of grace to the Gentiles. This man would have to break with the ingrained tradition of the Jews, who tended to be a clannish people. They would not mix with Gentiles, even refusing to eat with them or enter their houses. In fact, when a Pharisee walked down the street, he would hold his robes very tightly around him for fear that his garment might touch a Gentile. Should a Pharisee accidentally touch a non-Jew, he would go home, take a bath, wash his robes, and stay away from the temple that day. He considered himself unclean. Yet the man God needed to proclaim the good news would have to go out and live with the Gentiles and become one with them.

How interesting it is that God chose for this special task the Jew who was most zealous for the traditions of his fathers!

As Paul looked back, he could see how God's hand had been on his life from the very beginning. Since Greek culture had saturated the world, the man God chose had to be steeped in its customs and philosophy. Because he was going to be traveling extensively throughout the Roman empire and facing all kinds of perils, he needed to have Roman citizenship.

Therefore God arranged that Saul should be born a Roman citizen. How his citizenship was attained is not known, but it would definitely serve as a big advantage to Paul, saving him from some difficult and even life-threatening circumstances (*see* Acts 22 and 25).

Tarsus also enjoyed a strong Greek culture. Paul had more than just a small exposure to Hellenistic custom and thought; he was part of it. This made it possible for him to deal effectively with the Gentiles and to know the nuances of Greek thought. His background allowed him to communicate the truths of Jesus Christ to the Greeks.

At the same time, God needed a person who was thoroughly Jewish. When Paul was about 12 years old, his parents sent him to Jerusalem to study at the feet of Gamaliel, one of the great Jewish scholars of the day. There Paul became absorbed in Hebrew culture and tradition, mastering the Talmud and the Hebrew Scriptures. Paul grew extremely zealous for the law and sought to become righteous by keeping it to the best of his ability. He excelled among his contemporaries. To the Philippians he wrote, "If any other man thinketh that he hath whereof he might trust in the flesh, I more" (Philippians 3:4). Peter and the other disciples, with their backgrounds as fishermen or tax collectors, weren't prepared to understand the law as thoroughly as did Paul.

When the day finally came for God to reveal His grace to Paul on the Damascus Road, the apostle could instantly fit together the Scriptures of the Old Testament with the recent appearance of Jesus Christ. He began to look at the Messiah from a new point of view. Paul was the perfect choice to preach the gospel of grace, for if anyone had sought to be righteous by the law, it was Paul. Here was a man who could say, "Concerning . . . the righteousness which is in the law, [I was] blameless" (Philippians 3:6). He knew the futility of trying to be righteous by the law, so when he came to the glorious knowledge of Jesus Christ, he gladly embraced the new righteousness imputed to him through his faith in Jesus Christ.

Nothing Has Changed

Paul's story is dramatic, but don't imagine for a moment that this kind of divine preparation is unique to him or other New Testament saints. I can examine my own life, for example, and see that God separated me from my mother's womb for the work He had for me to do.

I look back and see momentous events that didn't seem so momentous at the time. Now I realize these incidents were the crossroads in my life that helped to shape and determine my destiny. Looking back, I can see the hand of God in each of these situations, although at those times I didn't realize God's hand was anywhere nearby. I thought God had deserted me. But now I see how God was working in every difficult circumstance of my life to prepare me for the work He had ordained for me. It is an exciting thing to recall some of the decisions I made at critical moments and realize that God's hand was leading me all along.

We sing, "All the way my Savior leads me." In hindsight, I can testify that God's hand was upon my life from the beginning. Sometimes God supernaturally intervened to protect me. He had a special work for me to do and He was fitting me for that work.

A few weeks before I was born my cousin died of spinal meningitis. My sister also was infected with this terrible disease. One day she went into convulsions so severe that my family thought she was dead. My mother rushed out of our apartment and up the street to the parsonage of a local church, where she laid my sister's lifeless body on the carpet. The pastor and my mother began to pray that God would bring my sister back to life. Her eyes had rolled back, her jaw had set, and there was no apparent pulse.

When my dad returned home from the pool hall a while later, a nurse was waiting for him. "You had better go find your wife," she said. "Your daughter is dying. She may even be dead by now." My father raced up the street to the parsonage to beat up the minister and take my sister to the hospital. He thought it was ridiculous to pray when you needed a doctor. But when he entered the home and saw my sister's condition, he realized it was too late. He fell on his knees, broken before God.

The minister told my mother, "Now, get your eyes off of your little girl. Just get your eyes upon Jesus and begin to look to the Lord." My mother—pregnant with me—lifted her face to God and said, "Lord, if You will restore to me my daughter, I will commit my life to You. I will serve You in whatever capacity You want." My sister was healed instantly. She began to cry, sat up, looked around, and wanted to go home. They took her home, completely healed.

A few weeks later I was born and the doctor announced, "You have a baby boy." My dad floated down the hall of the hospital shouting, "Praise the Lord, it's a boy!" At that time my mother prayed, "Thank You, Lord, for giving my daughter back to me. And the vow that I made to serve You, I will fulfill through my son."

From my earliest days, my mother planted the Word of God in my heart. As I was swinging out in the yard, she would help me memorize Scripture verses. When I was four years old she taught me how to read using the Bible. I spelled out the words I couldn't pronounce. She would later recount times when I didn't know all the letters and would do my best to describe them. She laughed as she remembered how I would call a "v" a "tent upside down." With patience and love, she nurtured and taught me the fear of God.

By the time I was seven years old I could name all of the books of the Bible and spell them. At bedtime, I never heard fairy tales, only Bible stories. Rather than Goldilocks and the three bears, I grew up with David and Moses. My mother taught me that when God was with you, you didn't have to fear anything or anybody. No giant could stand against you when God is with you.

I can't remember a time when I didn't know and love God. I have no kind of conversion testimony. There was a time when I made my public profession of faith and was baptized, but it seems that from my mother's womb I was separated unto God and unto the Word of God.

As I grew older, I decided on a career as a neurosurgeon and so began taking courses that would prepare me for that profession. Whenever I described my ambitions, my mother would just smile and encourage me. She never told me of the commitment she made for my life at the time of my birth.

During my teen years God changed my life at a summer camp where I made a commitment to the lordship of Jesus Christ. God impressed upon my heart that men had needs far greater than the physical. Ministering to physical needs provides temporary help, but ministering to spiritual needs helps people eternally. God called me to minister His healing to the spirit of man.

I thought my mom would be greatly disappointed when she learned her son was not going to be a doctor. I expected slumped shoulders and long faces when I announced to my family the change of direction for my life. But when I told my mother that I felt God calling me to the ministry and to Bible college, she just smiled and said, "That's fine, son." It amazed me that she didn't cry or get upset.

I went to Bible college, received my training, married Kay, and together we began our ministry. A short while before my mother died, she told me the story of my sister's apparent death and her promise to God which she vowed to keep through me. She was one of the most beautiful, godly persons I have ever known, a deeply spiritual woman and a tremendous example. I can now look back and see that even from my mother's womb I was separated unto God for the ministry He had in mind for me.

Did you know the same is true of you? If through faith you have placed your eternal destiny in the loving hands of Jesus Christ, you can be sure that God is at work shaping the events and circumstances of your life into a beautiful mosaic that will reveal His Son to the men and women around you. His hand is on you, as it has been since before you were born.

Called by Grace

It is so important to remember that God's hand is on us *by grace*. All of us were called *by grace*. As Paul said, "It pleased God, who separated me from my mother's womb, and *called me by His grace*" (Galatians 1:15, emphasis added). I don't deserve to be called to serve God. I don't deserve to be saved. I don't deserve to be in heaven. I deserve the hottest spot in hell.

Yet that is not what God has given me or the rest of us. God has graciously planned our lives and given each of us a special work to do. Some people are able to fulfill the plan of God for their life in just an hour's time; others of us are slow and plodding and it will take us a lifetime to fulfill God's ultimate purpose for us.

God has a special work for each of us to do and it is necessary that all of us be prepared for that work.

Remember Mordecai's question to Esther: "How do you know but that God brought you to the kingdom for such an hour as this?" (*see* Esther 4:14). The major purpose of God for Esther's existence was fulfilled in just a few days. God raised her up, brought her into the Persian court, and made her the wife of King Ahasuerus in order that He, through her intercession, might spare the Jews.

God has a special work for each of us to do and it is necessary that all of us be prepared for that work. Many of us will spend the majority of our lives in preparation before our day will come. We will fulfill the purpose of God for our life and then we will pass on. God's purposes for us will have been accomplished.

Wherever we find ourselves, God has a reason for placing us there. He has His hand upon our lives and upon each circumstance in our lives. We may be going through difficult trials, but hardships are necessary. God wants to develop in us the characteristics that will enable us to fulfill His plan for us.

God is working in each of us. We are His workmanship, His *poiēma* or masterpiece (*see* Ephesians 2:10). God will work in each of us according to His grace so that we might accomplish the work He

has ordained for us in His kingdom and for His
glory.

Beware the Snare

Satan knows that God's hand is on us and he
will try to use our weaknesses and inabilities to discourage us. The devil often puts unreasonable
demands upon us, making us think God is behind
them and prompting us to strive and struggle to
achieve a level of perfection beyond our capacity.

As Satan harasses and burdens us, many times
we fall into despair. We become extremely discouraged and we want to quit. But whenever we try
to fulfill a standard that God has not set for us, our
hearts grow heavy. And the results can be tragic.

A young boy with a physical handicap had been
attending our church. After every service he made
an effort to come up and talk to me. He had great dif-
ficulty speaking, yet I always admired his ability to
express himself. I also admired his intelligence;
his questions were good and insightful.

He was also extremely troubled, however, and
one day he tried to throw himself in front of a car on
a busy road in front of the church. He was brought
into the office and we prayed with him and called the
authorities. We felt for his own safety he needed to
be examined by doctors. He was taken to a hospital,
where he was examined and released.

It was clear he was suffering under a load of condemnation. "Chuck," he cried, "I just can't quit
smoking." I tried to tell him not to worry about it—
that his smoking did not make him a second-class
Christian. The following Sunday he was back at
church and told me God had dealt with him. He said
he had come to a place of real commitment, yet I

could tell he was troubled. Clearly, Satan was accusing him about a weakness in his flesh and tormenting him about his physical handicap.

One day this burden of discouragement and condemnation cost this young man his life. He jumped to his death off a balcony at a local high-rise hotel—all because he allowed the enemy to use his weaknesses to discourage him.

If only that young man had learned that we can't be more than the person God enables us to be! None of us ever achieves any value apart from the work of God's Holy Spirit in our lives. Thus, we are not to fret. We are not to condemn ourselves. We are not to berate ourselves constantly for our failures. We are only to acknowledge and recognize our weakness, to humbly say, "Lord, I know that I am weak. I need Your help. I turn this over to You and I ask You, Lord, to do for me what I can't do for myself." *And He will.*

All Are Welcome Here

The body of Christ is a beautiful thing. Every part of the body is vital and important. What a helpless and weird body it would be if it were all a mouth! God has made me a mouth in the body, but surely the whole body isn't a mouth. Many parts of the body are much more important than the mouth. How beautiful it is to see the body of Christ functioning as intended, with people from every walk of life and demographic group and background working together to serve God in unity!

God wants to reveal His Son in you, wherever you came from and wherever you are and in whatever you are doing. Let Jesus Christ shine forth through your life, your attitudes, your reactions, and your responses.

We used to sing a chorus in church, "Let the beauty of Jesus be seen in me, all His wonderful passion and purity. Oh, Thou Spirit divine, all my nature refine, till the beauty of Jesus be seen in me." This is more than just a beautiful chorus and a marvelous prayer. It should be the desire of each of our hearts: "Oh Lord, let Your beauty be seen in me." As David prayed, "I shall be satisfied, when I awake, with thy likeness" (Psalm 17:15).

By the Spirit, all of us—the lovely and the plain, the strong and the weak, the brilliant and the slow— are being changed into the likeness of Jesus. Together we are the objects of His grace. And together we shall all be satisfied on that glorious day when we awake in His likeness.

How could it be otherwise?

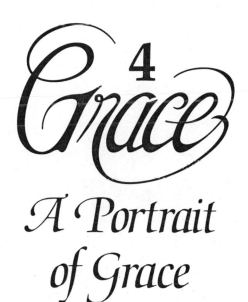

4
Grace

A Portrait
of Grace

I T'S ONE THING TO talk about grace in the abstract, but quite another to describe what it looks like. If "a picture is worth a thousand words," what kind of picture does grace make?

Perhaps the best picture of grace in the entire Bible is provided by an Old Testament character cited by several writers in the New Testament. Abraham is universally accepted as the father of those who believe. He gives us a clear picture of what grace is and does.

In both Romans and Galatians, the apostle Paul goes back to Abraham as the prime example of a man whom God accepted on the basis of his faith. In Romans 4:3, Paul wrote, "What saith the scriptures? Abraham believed God, and it was counted unto him for righteousness." The apostle uses the same example in Galatians 3:6,7, where he wrote, "Even as Abraham believed God, and it was accounted to him for righteousness, know ye therefore that they which are of faith, the same are the children of Abraham."

Rehearsing the Story

Genesis 15 tells us that Abraham and his wife, Sarah, were unable to have children. Yet God gave them a promise that through their seed, all nations of the earth would be blessed. Despite the improbability of it all, Abraham trusted God. Genesis 15:6 says, "And he believed in the LORD; and he counted it to him for righteousness."

As year after year rolled on and no baby came, however, Abraham and Sarah began to doubt whether God was going to follow through on His promise. So one day Sarah took matters into her own hands and suggested that Abraham impregnate her handmaid, Hagar. They would then raise the child as if it were their own. (How interesting that the idea of surrogate parenthood isn't as modern a development as we'd like to think!) Hagar conceived and gave birth to a son, who they named Ishmael. Yet when this child was 13 years old, God repeated His promise to Abraham. Abraham still had a hard time believing that God would give him a son with Sarah. He told God that the idea was nice, but really, Ishmael was already there—why not just bless him?

How encouraging that Abraham, a man the Bible calls the "father of all those who believe" (Romans 4:11), struggled to believe that the promise could be fulfilled through Sarah's seed! When the Lord repeated His promise to provide a son through Sarah, it was so incredible that Sarah laughed. Years later when the promise was fulfilled and Sarah gave birth, they named their son Isaac, which means "laughter."

As Isaac grew, his older brother Ishmael came to resent the attention lavished on this child of promise. At the party given to celebrate the weaning of Isaac, Ishmael stood at a distance, mocking his brother. When Sarah observed his spiteful attitude, she demanded that Abraham send away both him and his mother Hagar. She insisted that Ishmael would not share in the inheritance destined for Isaac.

Naturally, Abraham was crushed by this turn of events, but God assured him that He would take care of Ishmael. Abraham was to listen to Sarah and cast out the bondwoman and her son. It was clear that they could not inherit the promised blessing of God.

Painting the Picture

When Paul wanted to bolster his case for righteousness by grace through faith, he pointed his readers back to Abraham. He said the story of Abraham contained an allegory that could make his point clear. Traditionally, rabbis of Paul's time held that there were primarily two interpretations for every passage of Scripture. The first, called the *peshat*, referred to the plain and obvious meaning of the text. They also held that there was a hidden meaning to each passage (the *remez*). Some rabbis held to two additional types of interpretation: the *derash*, which involved allegorical meanings and anything not literal; and the *sod* ("secret"), which yielded an allegorical meaning. The drawback to these complex and often contradictory schools of thought is that they leave the average person confused and doubtful about the message of Scripture.

I believe the best focus is the plain and obvious meaning of the text. God is entirely capable of saying exactly what He means to say. So many have strayed

from the clear teaching of the Bible by pursuing spiri-
tualized, fanciful interpretations of Scripture. Let's
face it: With enough spiritualizing, we can take something as innocuous as Old Mother Hubbard and
develop a tremendous sermon out of that tale. Think
of the deep spiritual implications of this old woman
who went to the cupboard to get her poor dog a
bone. Why, we can picture her, trapped in the desola-
tion, discouragement, and emptiness of life because
the cupboard was bare. What a tragic day when all
our resources are gone!

With a little imagination we can create doctrinal
mountains out of the smallest molehill. The best rule
of thumb, then, is to avoid allegorical interpretations
unless Scripture itself gives us the basis for the allegory. In this case, by the inspiration of the Holy
Spirit, Paul draws an allegorical implication from the
life of Abraham which can be trusted:

> For it is written, that Abraham had two sons,
> the one by a bondmaid, the other by a free-
> woman. But he who was of the bondwoman
> was born after the flesh; but he of the free-
> woman was by promise. Which things are an
> allegory: for these are the two covenants;
> the one from the mount Sinai, which gendereth
> to bondage, which is Agar. For this Agar is
> mount Sinai in Arabia, and answereth to Jeru-
> salem which now is, and is in bondage with
> her children. But Jerusalem which is above is
> free, which is the mother of us all. For it is
> written, Rejoice, thou barren that bearest not;
> break forth and cry, thou that travailest not:
> for the desolate hath many more children than
> she which hath an husband. Now we, breth-
> ren, as Isaac was, are the children of promise

But as then he that was born after the flesh persecuted him that was born after the Spirit, even so it is now. Nevertheless what saith the scripture? Cast out the bondwoman and her son: for the son of the bondwoman shall not be heir with the son of the freewoman. So then, brethren, we are not children of the bondwoman, but of the free (Galatians 4:22-31).

The Significance of the Story

Paul tells us that these events are not only significant in a purely historical sense, but that they also illustrate the plight of those who try to inherit the blessings of God through works. Hagar and her son are a picture of those who try to be righteous before God by fulfilling the law. When Abraham and Sarah despaired of seeing the promise fulfilled, they turned to their own efforts, which brought only heartache and frustration. Since Ishmael was a product of the flesh, he serves as a type of those who are seeking to be blessed by human works. Isaac, on the other hand, is the child of promise, representing those who will inherit God's blessing through faith.

Interestingly, just as Ishmael mocked Isaac, those who live under the law today continue to deride those who choose to live by faith. Paul suggests that the pressure tactics of the Judaizers were prefigured in the conflict between these brothers. In like manner, those in his day who insisted on adherence to the law for righteousness were to be cast out. In A.D. 70 this allegory was fulfilled as Jerusalem was destroyed by the Roman legions under Titus. Those who persecuted men and women of faith were literally sent into exile.

---

*The freedom, the promise,
and the blessings of God
belong to all who seek
right standing with
God through Jesus Christ.*

Paul contrasts the sad end of the legalists with the wonderful future of the children of faith. Quoting Isaiah, he writes, "Rejoice, thou barren that bearest not; break forth and cry, thou that travailest not: for the desolate hath many more children than she which hath an husband" (verse 27). He means that these believers, gathered into the kingdom as a result of faith, were going to vastly outnumber all those who tried to reach God by their own works.

Just here the allegory comes into focus: "So then, brethren, we are not children of the bond-woman, but of the free" (verse 31). All those who belong to Christ will inherit the blessings of God and are the fulfillment of His promise to Abraham that in his seed all the nations of the earth would be blessed.

We have been blessed through the seed of Abraham, Jesus Christ. The freedom, the promise, and the blessings of God belong to all those who seek right standing with God through faith in Jesus Christ. As children of the promise and recipients of the unconditional love of God, we can now enjoy a wonderful consistency in our walk with Christ.

As the hymn so eloquently puts it, "Jesus paid it all. All to Him I owe; Sin had left a crimson stain, He washed it white as snow." When we appear before the throne of God, we will stand in awe of all Christ has done for us. As we see the power of the promises of God, none of us will say, "Through my own faithful and determined efforts, I have attained this glory." Instead we will bow our heads, overflowing with joy, and say, "Thank You, Jesus; You did it all! I knew You could save me. I knew that by my good works I could never save myself. Thank You, Lord."

A Key Question

Such was Abraham's faith. But the key question is, When did God proclaim this man righteous— when he was circumcised or before he was circumcised? The false teachers at Galatia were saying, "You can't be righteous unless you are circumcised." They insisted that a ritual was essential for salvation.

So when did God impute Abraham's faith for righteousness? Was it before or after he had received the rite of circumcision? It was *before*, not after! Abraham was accounted righteous before he knew a thing about this ritual. The declaration of his imputed righteousness is found in Genesis 15, while the rite of circumcision is not introduced until two chapters later. Righteousness was imputed to Abraham the moment he believed and trusted in God.

The same is true for you and me. At the moment we believe and trust in Jesus Christ, God imputes to our account righteousness—not on the basis of what we have done or what we are going to do, but simply on the basis of our belief in Jesus Christ.

As Christ is the Lord of heaven, the Son of God, and my own personal Savior, I will trust in Him. When I do, God says of me, "Righteous!" One day Jesus was asked, "What shall we do, that we might work the works of God?" Jesus replied, "This is the work of God, that ye believe on him who he hath sent" (John 6:28,29). If you want to do the work of

God, believe on Jesus Christ. That is the work of
God. That is what God requires of you.

But What Is Real Faith?

It is interesting that James—who writes an
epistle to kick some Christians in the pants to get
them off of their duffs and get them moving—also
uses Abraham as a picture of faith. His particular
concern is to show that faith without works is dead
(James 2:26). James says that Abraham's faith led him
to do certain things, and therefore God recognized
his faith: "Seest thou how faith wrought with his
works, and by works was faith made perfect? And the
scripture was fulfilled which saith, Abraham
believed God, and it was imputed unto him for righteousness: and he was called the Friend of God"
(James 2:22,23).

---

*Our actions must be in
harmony with what we
believe. Belief isn't
merely what we say;
belief is demonstrated by
what we do.*

In other words, true faith is more than a verbal-
ization. True faith leads to appropriate actions. If I
truly believe a certain thing, then my actions will be
in keeping with what I believe. I may vehemently
protest a belief in something, but if my actions are

inconsistent with my professed belief, then my belief must be called into question.

For example, I may say that I believe there is going to be a great stock market crash on Monday and that money is no longer going to be any good. The banks are all going to be closed, the savings and loans are going to shut their doors, and you will not be able to get your money out. Yet if I don't go down to the bank immediately and withdraw all of my deposits, you could rightfully say that I really didn't believe what I had said.

Our actions must be in harmony with what we believe or our belief can be called into question. Because Abraham truly believed that through Isaac his seed would be called, he was able to take his son up to the mountain, place him on the altar, and raise the knife. He was ready to bring the knife down because he believed that God had promised that through Isaac his seed would be called (Isaac did not at that point have any children) and he was willing to obey God in offering Isaac as a sacrifice. He knew that God would, if necessary, raise Isaac from the dead to fulfill his promise (*see* Hebrews 11:19). That is how much he believed the promises of God.

How much do *we* believe the promises of God? Many years ago I heard of a fellow who ran out of fuel in the middle of a blizzard and needed to ask a neighbor for some oil. The river that separated his house from his neighbor's was frozen over, so he got down on his hands and knees and reached out as far as he could on the ice, rapping with his knuckles to determine the ice's thickness. In this way he inched his way across the river, reaching out and tapping. Soon his knuckles were bloody. Just about the time he reached the far bank of the river, he heard a rumbling behind him . . . and saw a team of horses thundering across the river.

Some of us say, "I believe the promise of God," yet we are knocking to see if His promise will hold us up. We inch out so carefully. "I know God said He was going to supply all of my needs," we say, "but I'm not sure He will. That bill is due—and I am knocking to see if He is going to hold me. I sure hope His promise holds up!" In contrast, others venture right out on the promises of God. They have learned that God always keeps His promises, no matter how bad the circumstances appear. At one time, they may have been ice-tappers, too—but time after time they discovered that God is faithful. Eventually their belief was strengthened, and they began to act on their belief. All of us act out our true beliefs; they are demonstrated in our life.

Abraham's belief was demonstrated by his actions. Had he sat there and argued with God, he would not have truly believed. Imagine if he had said, "God, I can't offer Isaac. What do you mean, Lord? He is my son. You have promised that through him the nations of the world will be blessed. Lord, I can't do that." A lot of people think that merely saying something makes it a belief. But belief isn't merely what you say; belief takes action. It is demonstrated by what you do.

That is why James, citing the same passage from the Old Testament as did Paul, seeks to prove that faith without works is dead. To say you believe something and yet fail to live out that belief proves that you don't have real faith. True faith demonstrates itself in actions which are in harmony with the faith that is declared. Abraham believed God, and his belief worked itself out in actions that were in harmony with his belief. Therefore, God considered his faith as righteousness.

Abraham was not righteous because of what he did. He was righteous because of what he believed.

What he did was in harmony with what he believed. God took the belief and imputed righteousness to Abraham for his belief.

Get the Picture?

None of this means, of course, that our actions are always going to be perfect. As children of God who believe in Jesus Christ, we are engaged in spiritual warfare. Though our spirits are renewed in Christ Jesus, we are still living in these old corrupt houses, our bodies. My corrupted house makes strong demands upon me. I find at times that I am battling my flesh so that I do not do the things I really want to do. Sometimes my activities and actions are opposed to my faith in Jesus Christ.

But I can't live in that condition. I may stumble and fall, as does everyone, but I don't lie there. The Spirit won't let me lie there. He prompts me and helps me to stand up again. When I stumble or fall, God doesn't get out the eraser and blot out my name from the book of life. When you are trying to teach your son or daughter to walk, their stumbling doesn't prompt you to shout, "Get out of here, you brat. You are not *my* child, falling like that! I disown you." No, you pick up your child and say, "You're all right. Try it again. Come to daddy, now. Come on! Come on!" You encourage your child to try again and again.

You are God's child. He is trying to help you to develop a walk with Him. It is comforting to know that when we stumble and fall, He doesn't kick us out. He doesn't disown us. He doesn't say, "You are not My child anymore because you have stumbled!" Instead, He picks us up and dusts us off. He says, "All right now, try again."

Anyone who is born of God cannot live in sin. We cannot be practicing a life of sin. If we are, we are proving that we do not believe what we say we do. Abraham believed God and his actions followed his belief.

Of course, that doesn't mean that once Abraham committed his life to God in faith he never wavered in belief again. Far from it! Sandwiched around the Bible's declaration of Abraham's faith in Genesis 15:6 are two incidents that describe great lapses in his faith. Chapters 12 and 20 of Genesis describe how Abraham concocted lies designed to save his own skin rather than relying on God to keep him safe. Abraham could be an ice-tapper, too—but that wasn't the dominant characteristic of his life. He suffered occasional lapses, as we all do, but he didn't live in those lapses. He lived out his faith to such an extent that the Bible calls him a man of faith. Abraham's faith led him to act out his faith.

And yet, it was not his actions by which God determined his righteousness; his righteousness was determined by his believing. It is the same with us. Our faith must necessarily lead to a life of obedience and right actions, but it is not those right actions or our obedience that earn us right standing before God. The righteousness of Jesus Christ is imparted to us by faith.

By virtue of the fact that I believe in God and am trusting in Jesus Christ, I become a son of Abraham. I become a descendant, and thus the promises and covenant blessings that God gave to Abraham are mine as well.

This gospel of grace was preached long ago in Abraham. His life is a glorious picture of what grace is and does. It is far more beautiful than any painting hanging in the Louvre or in the Prado or in the Metropolitan Museum of Art. It is a stunning portrait of

God's love for a sinner who places his complete trust in Him—and the best thing of all about the picture is that we're right there in the background, with the word "blessed" emblazoned on our foreheads.

5
Grace

One Step
at a Time

YEARS AGO A CLOSE friend operated a delivery business to grocery stores. During his rounds he met the wife of a man who owned a small market. They began to kid around with one another and, before long, they were meeting regularly to drink coffee and to talk. They soon fancied themselves in love, left their families, and moved in together. That's when this man's wife, also a dear friend, called us and asked if we would pray for him.

Meanwhile, the minister of the church where our friends had been attending paid a visit to the man. The pastor told him that he had a vision of a black hearse and if the man didn't leave this woman and go back to his wife, they were going to carry him out of that room feetfirst. This heavy-handed approach only made the man more angry and entrenched him in his immoral decision. His wife then called me and asked if I would talk to him.

I agreed to go and found my friend living in a shabby garage apartment on the bad side of town. When I saw his filthy little home, I was struck by how much he had lost. His wife and daughters were beautiful people. His home was in a wonderful area. This man had sold his soul for a crust of bread. As he came to the door, a look of shame covered his face. He was very polite and invited me to come in and sit down. As I looked around at my friend's new life I thought, *Oh, God! How could he give up so much for so little?*

My heart was breaking because I loved this man. The sight of what he had fallen into tore me apart. I found myself unable to conceal my feelings, and much to my embarrassment I began to weep. I was overcome with grief, and when his lover emerged from the kitchen all I could do was sob. I finally got so embarrassed I said, "I'm very sorry. I know I came over to see you, but I just can't talk right now." I got up, left, and went home feeling like a fool. Here my good friend's wife wanted me to visit him and make an appeal for reconciliation, and all I could do was sit there and cry.

The next morning I received a phone call with news that left me in shock. My friend had returned to his wife and family just hours after my visit.

What did God use to achieve this miraculous healing of a fractured relationship? Not a holier-than-thou attitude, to be certain. His Spirit had created in me a spirit of meekness and brokenness that led to a joyful reconciliation. I thought I had blundered terribly—but I discovered that whenever we choose to walk in the Spirit, God delights to work powerfully in stunning and unexpected ways.

Walking in the Spirit is an amazingly practical proposition. It doesn't mean that we float through life with a halo over our head and an angelic smile on our face. We can be spiritually minded and still relate to people about earthly things. Some believers react so strongly against the pervasive worldliness of our culture that they lose the ability to communicate with their friends, relatives, and neighbors. Walking in the Spirit doesn't take us out of reality; it allows us to function in reality with optimum effectiveness.

Relationship First

Somebody once said, "The main thing is to keep the main thing the main thing." How true that is in the spiritual realm! While walking in the Spirit is an incredibly practical proposition, we must bear in mind that it's not the place we begin. *Relationship always precedes behavior.*

A great example of this principle is found in the book of Ephesians. The first three chapters all deal with relationship. Only then does the fourth chapter begin, "Therefore . . . walk worthy of the vocation wherewith ye are called." The relationship comes first because it provides the foundation for everything that follows.

If we try to walk without first establishing the proper relationship, we won't make it. Walking requires that we first acquire balance. This is true even in the physical realm. Before children take their first steps, they must learn how to keep their balance while sitting. Next they master the art of standing. Then they learn to wobble a little. And only after that do they develop the ability to walk.

In the book of Ephesians, Paul tells us that by understanding what it means to be seated with Christ we will begin to experience the power of God, which in turn will allow us to walk in a manner pleasing to Him. There is a definite progression here. First we must have a balanced relationship with God; then we can learn to walk.

At one time all of us lived after our flesh, obeying the desires of our flesh and our minds, and were alienated from God. But then God's grace transformed our lives and we began to enjoy delightful fellowship with the Lord. We continue to enjoy that deep fellowship as we allow God's Spirit to exercise control over our lives.

Walking Our Talk

There are many who claim to have a relationship with God, who throw around all the right Christian buzzwords and catchphrases, but who simply aren't walking with God in any practical way. It is crucial that we learn to "walk our talk." Our lives must be consistent with the calling, the blessings, and the profession we make concerning our new relationship with God.

Our mind is the battleground where we decide whether to live after the Spirit or after our fleshly desires.

The question is, How do we manage this? How do we avoid being carried away by the allure of the world? Paul had an answer in Galatians 5:16: "This I say then, *walk in the Spirit*, and ye shall not fulfil the lust of the flesh" (emphasis added).

The Greek word translated "walk" in this passage is a term used to describe the dominant characteristic of a person's life. If someone were to have a reputation as a real miser, he would be known as a person who "walked" in greed. If a person characteristically was concerned and helpful, he would be known as someone who "walked" in kindness.

To walk in the Spirit means that we allow the Holy Spirit to exercise control over our lives. Every day we are presented with the option of living after the Spirit or after our own fleshly desires. Our mind is the battleground where we will decide which will have dominion.

It is helpful to remember that God has designed the human mind to work much as a computer does. A computer can only produce that which has been programmed into it. In like manner, our minds are being programmed daily. If our input comes from the flesh, our lives will be characterized by the flesh. If we begin to program our minds with the things of the Spirit, our lives will begin to reflect the priorities of the Spirit.

How easy it is to fall into the trap of making a bold profession of a vital spiritual life when our number-one priority is seeking to please the flesh! Certainly the power that our fallen nature can hold over us is one of the biggest problems we face in life. How can we be free from the seemingly unconquerable bondage to the flesh?

The simple yet profound answer is this: *Don't fight the flesh, strengthen the Spirit!* Don't fight against the darkness; turn on the light.

To do this, we must first recognize that we have both a spiritual and a fleshly side to our nature. If we are to walk in the Spirit, we must feed the spiritual man. We all know what it means to feed the physical side of our nature. If I miss feeding my body, it is not subtle about reminding me of its needs.

Someone once told me that after three days of fasting, the hunger goes away. I have found the opposite to be true. Three days into a fast, my mind is busy dreaming of the most luscious concoctions imaginable. This is simply my body's emphatic way of reminding me that its needs must be tended to. And so we feed our bodies. We exercise and take vitamins so that we might grow strong physically.

Becoming strong in spirit requires a similar regimen. We must regularly consume the bread of life, the Word of God.

Taking in the Word

How ironic it is that our consumption of the Word is often the last thing we get around to. "Of course, I need to spend time in God's Word," we say, "but I just don't seem to have time right now." In essence, we are fasting in the Spirit. Our spiritual side often gets fed irregularly, spasmodically, and in an unbalanced way. We neglect a regular, systematic study of the Word for a "let's flip open the Bible and see what catches our eye" approach. Often we have no consistent practice of Bible study or personal growth. We end up dutifully feeding the areas of our flesh but neglecting the needs of the spirit. As a result, the spiritual man becomes weak and the flesh begins to dominate.

If I want my spiritual man to be strong, it only stands to reason that I must sow to my spirit. I can't be sowing to the flesh and hope that I'm somehow going to produce a spiritual crop. In order to walk in the Spirit, I must begin to feed the spirit. That means

I must make it a point to get more and more into the Word of God. Job said, "I have treasured the words of His mouth more than my necessary food" (Job 23:12, NKJV). It is important to see God's Word as the essential that it is. Jesus claimed that His words were spirit and life, so a regular, systematic time in God's Word is essential if we are to walk in the Spirit.

Communing with God

A high priority on prayer is another essential for experiencing the joys of walking in the Spirit. As we thrill to the excitement of communing with God, we find ourselves being strengthened in spirit. We become more and more conscious of the presence of God in all that we do and in every circumstance we encounter.

To walk in the Spirit simply means that we deliberately make God our constant companion.

Being aware of God's presence opens our understanding to a more full and developed worldview. I am convinced that one of our greatest needs is to become more and more aware of God's presence at all times. When Paul spoke to the Epicurean and Stoic philosophers in Athens as recounted in Acts 17, he declared that "in [God] we live, and move, and have our being" (verse 28).

Our lives can be remarkably transformed when we come to realize that God is with us continually. Losing sight of that fact can open the door to spiritual disaster. The farther God is removed from our consciousness, the more we are strongly drawn to the things that feed and please our fallen nature. When we stumble and fall we may point to many external factors to explain our behavior, but the root of our problem is a failure to keep God's presence in mind. The instruction to walk in the Spirit simply means that we are to deliberately make God our constant traveling companion as we move through the day.

When we walk in the Spirit, living in constant awareness of the presence of God, we no longer need others to nag and preach at us about living up to Christian standards. Our lives will be revolutionized as we keep the nearness and love of God in the front of our minds.

Turning Irritation into Joy

The way we think about even the most mundane things changes radically when we allow the Holy Spirit to rule our lives. Our outward circumstances may remain the same, but our attitude undergoes such a total transformation that we find joy even in things that used to irritate us.

We all have things to do that we find detestable. We go through a classic approach-avoidance conflict, knowing that while we hate to do these things, failing to do them will only worsen our situation.

I despise taking out the trash. Yet I know that if I don't do it, there will soon be a foul odor stinking up the porch. Therefore I bite the bullet and do the job. I would much rather be enjoying a bowl of chocolate-chip ice cream, but if I neglect my duty, soon the stench of decaying garbage will mix with the flavor of chocolate chips, and suddenly my desire for ice cream melts away.

Even in something as ordinary as this household chore, I have a choice. I can grumble about how much I hate hauling garbage, or I can seize the time it takes to do this job and commune with God. I can worship Him by whistling a tune of thanksgiving and love as I walk to the curb. As I draw near to God, I find myself thinking less about trash and more about His grace. I can sail through even the most distasteful task and not be perturbed by it if I set my mind on the things of the Spirit.

Consider waiting as another example. There are few things more aggravating than a red traffic light when you're in a hurry, knowing that you'll have to wait through a whole sequence of signals before you can get moving again.

But rather than getting tense, I have made it a practice to keep my Bible on the seat beside me. When I come to a red light and know I have some time, I'll start to read a portion of Scripture. The next thing I know the guy behind me is honking his horn. Time passes so quickly when I feed on the Word!

Walking in the Spirit becomes an exciting experience as we learn what it means to be in deep fellowship with God. We become more and more attuned to the things of God—from His presence within our hearts to the marvelous works of His creation.

Who's in the Lead?

Walking assumes movement. When we walk, we move from one place to another. We start out in one location and end up someplace else. Our destination depends upon the direction we take.

In a similar way, walking in the Spirit moves us from one spiritual place to another. We move from one level of maturity to the next as we listen to the Spirit and walk in the direction He instructs us to move—yet this is where we sometimes run into trouble.

When a thought or an inclination comes to our conscience, how can we discern whether the notion is from God? The Scriptures tell us that God writes His law on the fleshly tablets of our hearts (*see* Jeremiah 31:33; 2 Corinthians 3:3). God will plant an idea within my spirit, and my spirit will communicate it to my intellect. This is usually perceived as an idea, a thought, or as a sudden moment of inspiration. God will give us a desire as a means of communicating His will for our lives.

Unfortunately, I also have desires that come from my own fallen nature. My flesh has a way of injecting very strong thoughts and inclinations into my mind. At times it is difficult to discern whether a notion has come from God or from my flesh.

Some time ago I was faced with this dilemma as I was driving to a speaking engagement in Ventura, California. It was a spectacular day and the thought crossed my mind to take a detour off the more direct route and enjoy the beauty of the Pacific Coast Highway. Watching the surf and feeling the cool sea breeze is such a treat that I suspected the desire was of my own flesh, but I decided to indulge myself anyway.

As circumstances worked out, I realized that God had planned for me to take the Coast Highway. As I neared Malibu, I saw two hitchhikers standing by the road and I felt a strong inclination to pull over and give them a ride. As our trip north progressed, I had the opportunity to share Christ with this two-some.

The pair stayed in Ventura and the following

night attended the church where I was speaking. That evening they made a public confession of faith in Christ and have since become strongly established in that local fellowship. After the whole experience unfolded, I was able to look back and think, *Wow! That was beautiful. God directed me. The desire I had in my heart to take the Coast Highway had come from Him.*

Still, it is often difficult to determine when the Lord is speaking to our hearts. We often mistakenly think that God can lead us only in mystical or dramatic ways. *Surely if God speaks to me,* we think, *the place is going to shake, the lights will go dim, and my hair is going to stand on end.* God has never spoken to me in that way. When God speaks to me, He speaks to my spirit, which in turn communicates the message to my consciousness in such a natural way that it is tough to immediately discern whether it is truly God's voice.

I wish I could provide a formula or a simple, three-point test to identify God's voice, but if such a procedure exists, I haven't discovered it. I struggle in distinguishing the voice of the Spirit from that of my flesh, just as you do. I wish I could recommend some foolproof way of being certain we are hearing from God, but unfortunately, that is beyond my ability.

And yet, God hasn't left us in a confusing fog. He has sent His Holy Spirit to dwell within our hearts not only to guide us in particular circumstances but also to lead us into an understanding of the revealed truth of His Word. He will never lead us contrary to anything He has already declared in the Scriptures.

Understanding the Word

It is interesting to see how some people who

have yet to receive the Lord end up incredibly discouraged when they attempt to read the Bible. They see the tremendous influence the Scriptures have had on the lives of millions and its impact on western civilization, and they want to understand what it has to say.

Invariably, these people become bogged down and exasperated and the meaning of the Bible eludes them. This should not surprise us, because the Bible itself tells us that the natural man does not understand the things of the Spirit, neither can he know them, because they are spiritually discerned (*see* 1 Corinthians 2:14). On the other hand, the spiritual man understands all things, though he is not understood by others. Because we have become rightly related to God through Christ, His Holy Spirit can now unfold truth to our hearts. The Word of God becomes alive and understandable to us.

This continuing revelatory ministry of the Spirit is vital. It is amazing how often I can read through a chapter of Scripture and get nothing out of it. I find myself coming to the end of the chapter and saying to myself, "Now, what was it that I just read?" At this point, I will often stop and pray, "Lord, surely this chapter has something to say to me. Please open my understanding and allow Your Spirit to minister to me from Your Word." Then, as I reread the chapter, I am amazed at the truth that breaks forth on my heart.

During our Sunday-morning services at Calvary we usually have a responsive reading from the Psalms. By our third service, I end up seeing things in the Scripture text that hadn't occurred to me in our first hour. One of the verses will begin to minister to me in a very special and powerful way. This experience of being led into all truth is a vivid part of what it means to walk in the Spirit.

Press On!

Between the flesh, this fallen world system, and Satan himself, we face real hindrances to spiritual growth. But the counsel of Scripture is to press on for the prize of the high calling of God which is in Christ Jesus (*see* Philippians 3:14). Jesus said, "Strive to enter in at the [narrow] gate" (Luke 13:24). The Greek word translated "strive" is *agōnizomai*, from which we get our English word *agonize*. Make no mistake; it isn't easy or natural to walk in the Spirit. It takes genuine effort, devotion, and moment-by-moment concentration.

It can't be overemphasized that this is a choice each of us must make daily. When we choose to walk in the Spirit, the practical results can be breathtakingly beautiful. We will enjoy a wonderful depth and consistency in our fellowship with God. As the apostle John observed, "If we walk in the light, as he is in the light, we have fellowship one with another, and the blood of Jesus Christ his Son, cleanseth us from all sin" (1 John 1:7).

What's especially exciting about fellowship with God is that the more we experience it, the more we desire it. The more we are personally touched by the peace and fulfillment of intimate communion with the Father, the harder it is to live without it. When we find ourselves out of fellowship, an inner emptiness calls us back to prayer and the Word.

As we walk in the Spirit, we begin to enjoy the tremendous benefits of a close relationship with God. We feel a conscious sense of joy welling up within our hearts. We can whistle while we face the aggravating responsibilities of life because even in the midst of a dirty job, our joy is in the Lord. There is a sense of peace, a depth of understanding, a patience, a kindness, a gentleness that comes from walking in the Spirit. There is a strength and power to cope with the persistent desires of the flesh. We suddenly are able to see the big picture and find the wisdom to deal with our fallen nature in a realistic and rational way. As Paul summed it up, "To be carnally minded is death; but to be spiritually minded is life and peace" (Romans 8:6).

How could we fail to be drawn with all our hearts to the glorious new life which Gód freely offers to us in His grace? A life strengthened by the Spirit— with joy, love, and peace flowing through us—is exactly what we passionately desire.

But in order to experience this blessing, we must choose to walk in the Spirit. We must come to God and ask Him to plant a greater desire for prayer, for time in the Word, and for fellowship with Jesus in our hearts. We must pray for the grace to seek first the kingdom of God and His righteousness. It is then that we will know tremendous victory over even our most besetting sins, and it is then that the Spirit of God is able to use us in the most extraordinary ways.

Even when all we can do is blubber.

6

Grace

A Garden,
Not a Factory

H AVE YOU EVER CONSIDERED the vast difference between "works" and "fruit"? "Works"
suggests a factory complete with pressures, deadlines,
and the constant need to produce. But "fruit" pic-
tures a peaceful, tranquil garden, a place where we
are inclined to stay and drink in the beauty while we
enjoy each other's company.

It's important to realize that God doesn't come to
His factory looking for products. He comes to His
garden to enjoy its fruit. The gospel of grace invites
us to leave behind the smog and pressure of a factory-
like life of works and instead bear the fruit that God
desires to see in the garden of our lives.

The Natural Result of Relationship

Galatians 3:2,3 is a critical passage for those who desire to live in a way that pleases God. Paul writes, "This only would I learn of you, received ye the Spirit by the works of the law, or by the hearing of faith? Are ye so foolish? Having begun in the Spirit, are ye now made perfect by the flesh?"

Notice the apostle is comparing two things:

- the Spirit, which is related to faith;

- works, which are related to the flesh.

Whenever we get into the realm of works, we are dealing with the flesh. Whenever we are in the realm of the Spirit, we are dealing with faith. The Spirit and faith are related, as are works and the flesh.

Someone may say, "But Chuck, we must do works for the Lord." No, we mustn't. There is not one thing that I can do in my flesh that will please God. On the other hand, faith always produces fruit.

If you are involved in works, then you are relying on the flesh. But if you are walking by faith with Jesus Christ, the Spirit is producing fruit in your life. Fruit isn't something you are generating because you think you have to; fruit is the natural result of relationship.

Look at the luscious fruit hanging on a peach tree. The peaches aren't out there struggling and working day by day trying to get ripe; all they have to do is hang in there. Ripening is the natural product of relationship. As long as they are abiding, they are going to bring forth sweet fruit.

This is true of our own experience as well. If we are truly abiding in Christ—which is a position of faith—then fruit will come forth from the relationship. If there is no fruit in my life, then the relationship must be questioned and even challenged.

That is why Paul tells us, "Examine yourselves, whether ye be in the faith; prove your own selves. Know ye not your own selves, how that Jesus Christ is in you, except ye be reprobates?" (2 Corinthians 13:5). Jesus told us that there is such a thing as a wolf in sheep's clothing. You can look like a Christian, act like a Christian, and talk like a Christian—but grandma, what big teeth you have! You may have all the outward appearances of a sheep but in reality be a wolf.

So how are we going to know who's who? Jesus said, "By their *fruits* ye shall know them" (Matthew 7:20, emphasis added).

We are called to examine our lives in order to determine what kind of fruit we're bearing. If the fruit is bad, then there is something wrong with our relationship, which means there is something wrong with our faith. A vital relationship of faith in Jesus Christ *will* bring forth fruit—without fail.

Our Big Mistake

One of our biggest problems is that we tend to be more interested in what we do than in what we are, while God is more interested in what we are than in what we do. He looks for fruit; we try to produce works.

Sadly, through the years we have all heard things like, "You ought to be doing these works for the Lord; you ought to be doing that work for God." We are always being exhorted and pressed into works for the kingdom. So we get out and start doing a work for God because the pastor or the committee has asked us to do it.

Maybe it is calling on visitors to the church when God hasn't called us to be a caller. I know some people who are petrified by visiting the homes of strangers. When they go to a door and knock, they're fervently praying, "Lord, please don't let them be home tonight." Visitation isn't natural for them. It is a forced effort, a work of the flesh, which they soon come to resent. They hate it and begin to drag their heels. So the committee chairman calls them up and says, "We missed you last Tuesday in our calling night. We want to make sure you are there next Tuesday night." They grudgingly respond, "Okay," and the downward spiral continues.

That's how you get pushed into molds for which God did not create you. You are forced into unnatural positions and you begin to chafe under your service to God. But God does not want you to give Him anything that you are going to gripe about. God can't stand "Christian griping." It's an insult to Him. Even I hate it when people gripe about what they have done for me. It makes me feel stupid and foolish. Who asked them to do it, anyhow?

If there's something you just don't want to do, don't do it. Don't go out and do some magnanimous deed and then gripe and complain about it. You would be better off to do nothing.

Leave the calling to those who love to do it. There are people who are thrilled to talk to strangers. They get bored just sitting at home and they can't wait to strike up conversations with people they've never met. That is their nature. It's *natural* for them— and that is the key.

When it is natural it is in the realm of fruit; when it's pressured it is in the realm of works. God always equips us to do whatever He has called us to do, and it will be natural for us to do it.

Many people feel like second-rate Christians because they can't do what others can. They run into a believer who says, "This past week, praise the Lord, I witnessed to five people and all five of them received Jesus." *Oh man,* thinks the person not blessed with the gift of evangelism, *I am a horrible witness to the Lord. I didn't witness to anybody. I am such a failure.* He is made to feel guilty because he wasn't out collaring people and asking them if they knew the four spiritual laws.

Why are some people so effective in evangelism? Because it is natural for them. God has endowed and equipped them for the work. Not everybody in the body is the mouth, however, and the mouth couldn't operate effectively unless there was a brain behind it and feet to carry it where it needed to go. We should not feel guilty because we do not have the same ministry or effectiveness as others. The body works as a unit, and God is the one who has assigned each of us our place in the body.

God wants you to do what He has naturally endowed you to do. The fruit of the Christian life blossoms from you naturally as you abide in Jesus Christ through your faith in Him. Jesus said, "Herein is my Father glorified, that ye bear much fruit" (John 15:8). God wants you to be extremely fruitful for Him. That fruit can come forth only as you abide in Christ—and that is a position of faith.

No Such Thing as Fleshly Faith

Matthew's Gospel tells us that one day many people will come to Jesus, telling Him of all the works they did for Him, and the Master will reply, "I never knew you" (Matthew 7:23). The Lord doesn't recognize works of the flesh; He never has.

Remember when God said to Abraham, "Take now thy son, thine only son Isaac...and offer him there for a burnt offering upon one of the mountains which I will tell thee of" (Genesis 22:2)? The Lord's comment sounds a little odd—after all, Abraham *did* have another son, Ishmael, who was at least 14 years older than Isaac. What did God mean, "Take now thy son, thine *only* son"?

The answer is, Ishmael was a work of the flesh. He was not the son of promise; he was not the son of faith. Ishmael was a product of the flesh. God refused to recognize Ishmael because he was the work of the flesh. God recognized only His work of the Spirit, Isaac, the child of faith. Therefore He said to Abraham, "Take now thy son, thine *only* son Isaac."

God never recognizes or rewards the works of our flesh. On the other hand, He jealously desires that the fruit of the Spirit be increasingly characteristic of our lives.

The fifteenth chapter of John explains how believers bear fruit. Jesus said, "Abide in me, and I in you. As the branch cannot bear fruit of itself, except it abide in the vine; no more can ye, except ye abide in me" (John 15:4). Jesus placed the emphasis not upon what we *do*, but upon what we *are*. What comes forth from our lives is the result of our relationship with Him. We can't have a true, right relationship with the Lord without bringing forth fruit. If there is no fruit—for "by their fruits ye shall know them"— then we had better reexamine our relationship.

Renegade Fruit Inspectors

God did a marvelous work in your life by His Holy Spirit. When you were still a sinner, God loved you. And when by faith you called out to Him, He justified you of every wrong thing you had ever done. God wiped your slate clean. He obliterated the past so thoroughly that He made it as though it never existed. That is what the term "justified" means.

The moment you received Jesus Christ by faith—before you paid one penny tithe, before you did one thing—God took all of the black marks against you and wiped them out. Because of your simple belief in Jesus Christ as your Savior and Lord, God justified you of all your past. Because of your belief, God imputed to your account the righteousness of Jesus. Your relationship with Him began by believing.

This is all very basic, but somehow we often forget it. Sometimes believers criticize other believers or find fault. They say, "Do you know what they are doing? This is terrible. They call themselves Christians, yet they are doing this and that. They are not living up to the standard—why, they even go down to the beach. That is horrible!"

Now, what are such believers doing? They have set themselves up as judges. They have become renegade fruit inspectors. They are judging the quality of another man's servant. Paul had something to say about that; he wrote, "Who art thou that judgest another man's servant? To his own master he standeth or falleth" (Romans 14:4).

It is much easier to please God than man. To please God, we only need to believe in Him and trust in Him. That is the gospel of grace.

If you were serving me, I might judge your service. I might say, "You are a lousy servant. I don't know why I keep you around." If you were doing something that displeased me, I would be the one to tell you, "Look, I don't like the way you're drying the dishes; you are leaving too much water on them and you're putting them away still wet. I don't like to get a glass out of the cupboard that still has moisture in it. That is where germs are bred. Now dry them completely."

On the other hand, I might say, "You are a wonderful servant. You do such great work! It is a pleasure to have you with me!" In either case, I would be the one to judge your service, not an outsider.

The truth is, I am not your master and I can't direct how you are to serve. You must stand before your own master and I can't judge your service. I can't say, "What a lousy servant you are." I have no right to judge your service to God. God is the one you are serving, and before your master you either stand or fall. Paul goes on to say, "God is able to make him stand" (Romans 14:4).

Don't worry that some people can't see how you're ever going to make it. I have found that God has been much easier to please than man. It is an exercise in futility to try to please everybody. Even if you manage it, someone is going to fault you because you are a people-pleaser. It's just not possible to please everybody.

What's beautiful is that we don't have to please everybody. All we have to do is please God. And what do we have to do to please Him? Just believe in Him and trust in Him. We don't please God by all of our works and feverish activities. We please God when we believe in Him and trust in Him. That is the gospel of grace.

It's My Pleasure!

Faith pleases the Lord and *faith* produces relationship. The relationship produces the fruit. I don't just sit and be pure and holy and righteous and smile and be sweet and show love all day long. I am caught up in activities, but activities which are not work. It is fantastic to be able to say, "You know, I am doing exactly what I want to do; in fact, I'm doing what I love to do!" It isn't a work, it isn't a favor, it is simply something I enjoy.

Years ago when I served in a denomination I would go to conventions and see some of my buddies. We would go out for dinner and I would start talking about a scripture that the Lord had opened up to my heart. "Oh, come on, Smith—shop talk," they'd say, and change the subject. I would reply, "What do you mean, 'shop talk'? This is my life! There is nothing I would rather talk about. There is nothing more exciting to discuss."

When you are doing what you love to do, it is not a work. You are not in a shop. You are not laboring in a factory. Your activity is the fruit of relationship.

When the love of God fills your heart, all you want to do is talk about Him: His Word, His goodness, His love. You don't go around looking for brownie points just because you have been doing what you like to do. You don't look to be rewarded for what is natural to you (even though God *will* reward you for the fruit that comes forth from your life). You do it because you want to do it, because it is your nature to do it, because God has put it in your heart to do it. The fact is, you feel as if you would die if you didn't do it.

"For the love of Christ constraineth me," wrote

Paul (2 Corinthians 5:14). "Woe is unto me, if I preach not the gospel!" (1 Corinthians 9:16).

I am sure all of us have had experiences like Jeremiah, who was thrown into a dungeon for declaring the word of the Lord to Israel's kings. As he was sitting in the dark he said, in effect, "That's it; I am through. God, here is my resignation. Don't ever ask me to speak in Your name again. I am not going to do it. Don't lay Your word upon my heart anymore. Lord, I am through, I have resigned. Do You understand? It is over. I'm never going to speak again in the name of the Lord. You treat me like this and let me get thrown in a dungeon. You don't take care of me. But it's all right; I am through!" (*see* Jeremiah 20:9).

Jeremiah was stewing. He was angry. Yet he soon confessed, "But his word was in mine heart as a burning fire shut up in my bones, and I was weary with forbearing, and I could not stay" (verse 9). He could do nothing *but* speak. He had to speak. He didn't have to force himself as if it were a work; in fact, he tried to force himself not to speak, but spoke anyway. Why? It was natural; it was the fruit of his relationship.

Griping Is Not a Fruit of the Spirit

God does not run factories; He grows gardens. He is not interested in your works; He desires to enjoy your fruit. He does not want you to depend upon your flesh; He calls you to rely upon His Spirit.

As Paul reminds us, having begun in the Spirit, we cannot be made perfect in our flesh (*see* Galatians 3:3). We cannot add works to our faith and improve the relationship, even though many people endeavor to do exactly that.

A Garden, Not a Factory

So many times people begin by believing in the Lord, loving the Lord, serving the Lord, and having a glorious time. The joy of the Spirit is theirs. Then some brethren show up and begin to lay heavy trips on them. "Hey brother, if you are really a Christian, you need to be doing this. How come you guys are doing that? Man, you mean you guys call yourselves Christians? Why, you don't even do this." They start laying down all of these heavy requirements so that Christianity becomes a grind. It ceases to be natural and a delight and begins to be a chore, a job, a work.

When will we learn? *We cannot improve on the righteousness given to us by God.* Any works-based relationship soon becomes a grind in which we lose the joy of our relationship with the Lord. Suddenly it's a duty, an obligation, an onerous task. Before long, we begin griping. The joy of the Lord departs from our walk. We no longer enjoy freedom, but labor under a yoke of bondage. We think, *I had better say my prayers tonight, or I will really be in trouble. Oh, but I am so tired. I don't want to get out of bed. I suppose I'll have to, but—oh, man, it's so cold!*

I am sure God says, "Oh, shut up and go to sleep! Don't bother Me in that kind of a mood. Who asked you to call, anyway?"

You might think that if anyone should have mastered this lesson, it would be ministers of the gospel. Yet there are men who would have us believe they minister the things of the Spirit by the works of the flesh. They will describe what great consecration it takes to have their kind of ministry—what tremendous personal sacrifices a person must make to have such power. They will tell of their commitment and their fasting and their consecration and will lay it all out as though their works have achieved for them some level of spirituality that moved God to entrust them with His power. God can't trust everybody with this power, they say, but they have earned it. Oftentimes they actually say things like, "I went into the other room, closed the door, and said, 'God, I am not going to come out of here until I have the power.' And I stayed in there and fasted and prayed until I got it." They speak as though their righteousness earned them God's favor. But it didn't; it was only a work. And God will never honor or recognize a work of the flesh.

Paul said, "Have ye suffered so many things in vain? If it be yet in vain. He therefore that ministereth to you the Spirit, and worketh miracles among you, doeth it by the works of the law, or by the hearing of faith?" (Galatians 3:4,5). A true minister gives all the glory to the Lord. "Let your light so shine before men," Jesus said, "that they may see your good works, and glorify your Father, which is in heaven" (Matthew 5:16).

We're All Invited

The works of God are not wrought because of our righteousness. They are wrought by grace through faith. And that means that any of us can do them. You don't have to be some specially anointed kind of instrument.

Let your life be as a garden
where God can come
to enjoy the fruit you
are producing as you
abide in Christ.

James says that Elijah was a man of passions just like us (*see* James 5:17). He became discouraged, he got upset, he got angry, he blew it. Yet he prayed and it didn't rain for three years. Elijah was not some superholy kind of prophet. He wasn't a mystic. He was a person exactly like us, with the same kind of feelings we have—the same kind of discouragements. Yet God listened to him because of his faith.

That same potential is yours. All it takes is believing the Lord and trusting in Him.

Since you've begun in the Spirit, you must continue in the Spirit. Having begun in faith, you must continue in faith. Don't degenerate into works; don't let your Christian experience become a bore. Don't become a factory worker, but let your life be as a garden where God can come to enjoy the fruit you are producing as you abide in Christ by faith.

7
Grace

Believing for
the Blessings

S OME MISTAKES just won't go away.
    Consider the error that tripped up the church
at Galatia some 2,000 years ago. Somehow, it's still
going strong today. Despite what Paul said about it,
to this day a lot of teachers promote the idea that the
Holy Spirit is received by the works of the law. How
tragic it is that one of the greatest stumbling blocks to
experiencing the fullness of God's blessing and
power is a doctrine picked up in church! We hear that
if we want the Holy Spirit to come into our lives, we
had better clean up our act. We must get rid of every
bit of impurity in order to be worthy of blessing.

    Although such teaching is very sincere, it is sin-
cerely wrong. The essence of such preaching is that
we must be made righteous by our own conduct and
efforts, and only then might God condescend to touch

us. It was this same misguided teaching that kept me from receiving God's best for so many years.

Faithful but Frustrated

As a child growing up in a Pentecostal church, I earnestly desired what was termed the baptism of the Holy Spirit. I went to many "tarrying meetings" and quite often accompanied my father to the Saturday night men's prayer meetings. There I would wait upon the Lord and pray that God would fill my life with His power.

I dearly loved the Lord and I desired all of the power of God that I could possibly obtain. But something was getting in the way. For many years I thought some secret sin was holding me back. And it was—but not at all the kind of sin I imagined. My problem was not lust, or greed, or some all-consuming habit. My problem was self-righteousness.

You may think it strange that someone so young would struggle with spiritual pride, but I did. I memorized Scripture. I could recite the books of the Bible and spell them. I could quote entire chapters of God's Word. I never went to a show. I never smoked a cigarette. I never went to dances. The church I attended taught that all of these things were sinful, so I avoided them religiously.

Many times I saw the preacher's son pick up cigarette butts and smoke them, but I wouldn't do it. My other buddies in church might go to the matinee every Saturday, but I never would. I was going to be *holy*.

Then what was so terribly wrong? God was blessing my buddies, even when they were smoking cigarette butts! *Lord, You know I am more righteous than they are*, I thought. *I've never done any of those evil things. Why bless them and not me?* I had a terrible struggle.

It got worse when I heard people give testimonies of how they were waiting for the filling of the Holy Spirit. As they waited upon God, the Lord showed them the pack of cigarettes in their pocket. The moment they pulled out the cigarettes and laid them on the altar, God apparently filled them with the Holy Spirit.

I was trying to earn God's blessing, but I was never good enough. It never occurred to me to just ask God in simple faith.

Perhaps my problem was that I never had a pack of cigarettes in my pocket to be lain on the altar. So instead I would mentally list my sins from that week and think, *Now Lord, I got mad at my brother this week. Lord, please forgive me for getting mad.* Then I would wait for Him to fill me with the Spirit. But He didn't.

Countless times I heard speakers say, "You know God won't fill an unclean vessel. He is the *Holy* Spirit. Therefore you must be a holy vessel." So I would do my best to be holy. I confessed to God everything I could think of (and even some things that I never did, just in case).

I would rake over the coals of my conscience time and again. I committed and recommitted my life to God. I gave up every small, questionable activity I could find and sacrificed precious things I loved, all in a futile effort to become holy and righteous enough for God's Spirit to fill my life. I was frustrated and stifled in my walk with Christ.

Finally in desperation I said, "All right Lord, I will go to China as a missionary. Please fill me with your Holy Spirit." He didn't. I promised the Lord that I would go to China, Africa, South America, and India. Still He didn't.

All that time I was endeavoring to receive the filling of the Holy Spirit by works—by becoming righteous through keeping the standards I had set up. I was trying to receive the Spirit by the works of the law. I tried every trick I knew, earnestly hungering and desiring to be filled by God and to receive His gifts. I don't know how many nights I agonized before Him, wondering why He never blessed me.

I was convinced some righteous plateau had to be reached before God would bless me. I believed that the moment I could achieve that high plateau, the Holy Spirit would fill me. And yet I was troubled by what I saw happening around me. How could people come off of the street and receive Jesus Christ as their Savior, stinking of booze and nicotine, and be baptized in the Holy Spirit right then and there? Yet they were.

It just wasn't fair. Here I had been walking with the Lord, serving Him all the way along, and they got blessed and I didn't. I couldn't understand the discrepancies of God. It was impossible for me to harmonize the teaching I had received with what I saw happening.

If only I had understood God's grace! I would not have waited all those years to receive the empowering of the Holy Spirit. As I began to read and understand the Word of God, eventually I came to the text where Paul asks, "Received ye the Spirit by the works of the law, or by the hearing of faith?"

(Galatians 3:2). Suddenly I realized this was a rhetorical question. The obvious answer was that they had received the Holy Spirit by the hearing of faith.

I was flabbergasted. I had never been taught such a thing. I had been trying on my own to become holy enough or righteous enough, but of course I never managed to become good enough to earn the filling of the Holy Spirit. It never occurred to me to ask in simple faith. I was sure God needed my help.

That day I put aside all my self-righteous efforts and simply said, "Lord, I am going to receive from you now the gift of your Holy Spirit." And I did, at that very moment. *Stupid me!* I thought. *I could have had this years ago if only I had known. If only I had been taught!*

Oh, what I lost in those lean years because of a teaching that emphasized obedience to rules and codes! We receive the indwelling, filling, and empowering of the Holy Spirit by trusting and believing in Jesus Christ as our Lord and Savior, not by keeping some external code. That is why I repeat this simple yet powerful message over and over, emphasizing God's grace, love, mercy, and goodness to us undeserving sinners.

Blessings for the Taking

Once I began to understand the Word, I saw that it wasn't my righteousness or ability to reach some plateau of holiness that makes me worthy of God's blessing. God blesses me when I simply trust in Him for His blessings. The longer I live, the more I realize how undeserving and unworthy I am of God's touch. He wants to bless me not because I am good and holy and pure, but because that is His nature. He enjoys blessing His children.

Did you know there is only one thing holding back God's blessings from your life? They're not withheld because you haven't been faithful in your devotions this week. They're not kept back because you've failed in some area of your life. Everyone fails. The only thing holding back God's blessings in your life is your own refusal to trust Him for those blessings. *The blessings of God are available to anyone who simply believes Him and trusts Him for those blessings.*

Don't come to God on the basis of your own righteousness or goodness. You'd be a fool to want to rob the Lord of the good work He wants to do in your life! The only attitude acceptable to Him says, "I'm a failure and I don't deserve it—but please, Lord, go ahead and bless me anyway."

Once I realized that the blessings of God were mine through simple faith in Him, I came to experience His blessing ever since. I have been given so much and received so much from God that it is impossible to keep track of all the blessings. I have come to a door that is never closed. When I was coming in my own righteousness, the door was closed most of the time. But now that I come to God on the basis of His love, that door is never closed.

God *always* loves us. His love for us doesn't change from day to day. He doesn't love us more today than He loved us yesterday. God's love isn't like that. God's love for us is constant; it never varies. His love for us is not predicated upon us; it is predicated upon Him and His nature of love.

God is love. He loves you and keeps loving you even when you are a rank sinner. Even when you were rebelling against Him, shaking your fist in His face and saying, "I hate you, God!" He loved you then. And He loves you now. Because God loves us, He wants to bless us. His blessings are not dependent upon our goodness, our righteousness, or our faithfulness. The blessings of God depend solely upon His desire to bless us. Our part is simply to receive and believe Him for His blessings. Remember Paul's rhetorical question? "Received ye the Spirit by the works of the law, or by the hearing of faith?" Did you become so righteous that God finally decided, "Well, he is righteous enough now, so I guess I will have to fill him"? No! We are no more righteous now than the first day we believed.

You can't imagine the blessing and power that God is eager to impart to you if you will just believe and trust Him for it. We are so often like the foolish Galatians. Why would we be so foolish as to return to a legal relationship when we can relate to God in a love relationship? Don't be a fool and demand what you think you deserve, because you deserve death. All of us do, for all of us sin.

God wants to bless you *now* because He loves you. God wants to bless your life, and the avenue to that blessing is your faith.

You Can't Mean Me!

Some of you reading this may believe that God can't possibly bless you because you have failed Him too much or because you are too weak or because you have done something terribly wrong. Perhaps you have a chronic problem with a vile temper or a wandering eye. You wonder, *How can God bless me when I yell at my kids? How can God bless me when I am so rotten? How can God bless me when I am this or that?* Your problem is that you are looking for a blessing on the basis of your own performance. You are trapped in the kind of thinking that says, "When I become so good and so perfect, then He can bless me."

But that is so misguided!

We must get it into our heads that God wants to fill our lives with the Holy Spirit the moment we say, "Lord, I really desire to have this power and I ask You to fill me."

But I must warn you. It is undeniable that at precisely this point, spiritual warfare erupts. When you pray for God's filling, instantly Satan will begin to throw all kinds of lies and accusations into your mind. He will distract you. He will make you feel guilty or unworthy. "What are you doing, asking God for that?" he'll sneer. "You should be ashamed of yourself. You have no right! Look at what you are. Look what you have done. How could God possibly fill you with His Holy Spirit?"

Ironically, many times Satan will use *Christian* people to deliver this lie. Any person on a self-righteous trip will inevitably heap blame on you. "It's your own fault, you know," he'll announce. "If only you had a little more faith. If only you were a little more spiritual. If only you were a little more like me." A little of such spiritual bombardment, and many of us decide to retract the whole thing. "Forget it, Lord," we say.

God wants you to experience His love, His touch, His power, and His anointing.

What a tragedy! I know I don't deserve the blessings of God, but God doesn't bless me because I deserve it. God blesses me on the basis of His love toward me and of His grace toward me in Christ

Jesus. That is the basis of the blessing—not my goodness, not my righteousness, and not my perfection. If
we could just get this through our tender skulls, we'd
start being blessed like we can't imagine.

The blessings are there. God wants to bless you. All
you have to do is simply believe Him to bless you,
though you know full well you don't deserve it. The
blessings don't come because of your works, they
come because of your belief—because you trust and
believe God will bless you.

Failure to grasp this truth is exactly why a lot of
people have real problems in their Christian experience. "I don't know why God has blessed him—
he smokes cigars!" someone says. "Why, I don't do
that. Yet look at all his blessings! I can't understand
why God blesses people who smoke cigars." But
of course, God's blessings are not predicated on
smoking habits. They're only predicated upon our
believing God to bless us because we are God's children.

God *wants* to bless His people today. The eyes of
the Lord go to and fro throughout the entire earth to
show Himself strong on behalf of those whose
hearts are perfect toward Him (*see* 2 Chronicles 16:9).
Just turn your heart toward God, believe in His
Word, and trust that He will do as He promises. Say,
"Lord, bless me now." And receive it.

I know that such freewheeling grace is almost an
affront to us. The moment I say, "Oh, Lord, lay a real
blessing on me. I really want a fantastic blessing
tonight," my mind objects: *What do you mean, asking
God for a blessing? With what you were thinking this after-
noon, how can you ask God to bless you?*

It is so hard for us to repudiate the idea of
deserving a blessing. Simply to believe and expect
God to bless us—though we have been failures and
don't deserve it—is extremely difficult for us. But

when we finally get over that barrier and come to expect God to bless us simply because He has promised to bless us, there is nothing that can stop His blessings from touching our lives.

The Blessing of Abraham

And what blessings they are! The same blessings which God promised to Abraham are ours because we are children of Abraham. Listen to just three of the promised blessings:

- "Fear not, Abram: I am thy shield, and thy exceeding great reward" (Genesis 15:1).

- "I will make thee exceeding fruitful" (Genesis 17:6).

- "I will establish my covenant between me and thee and thy seed after thee in their generations for an everlasting covenant, to be a God unto thee, and to thy seed after thee" (Genesis 17:7).

All these blessings, and more, are yours. Because God sees you in Christ, the righteousness of Jesus is imparted to you. That and that alone is the basis upon which God blesses you, thoroughly and completely.

The gospel of grace insists that even though you don't deserve it, God wants you to experience His love, His touch, His power, and His anointing. God has given to each person a measure of faith. Exercise it, use it, and it will develop. Just simply believe, trust in the Lord, and expect God to bless you.

Never forget that the blessing of God's Spirit in our lives is not granted to us because one day we became holy enough to deserve His blessing. It came to us when at last we saw the light and simply believed God to keep His Word. Our works of righteousness had nothing to do with it.

God's ways haven't changed a bit. The blessing of Abraham comes to us all through simple faith in our Lord Jesus. Our part is merely to believe Him for His blessings.

And, come to think of it—that's quite a blessing in itself.

8
Grace

The Struggle Begins

N OT LONG AGO I received a letter from
a young man who told me of his intense
struggles with the flesh. He described his discourag-
ing track record of defeat after defeat, almost echoing
Paul's cry in Romans 7:24: "O wretched man that I
am! Who shall deliver me from the body of this
death?"

It was easy for me to relate to his experience.
All of us have suffered through similar tough times
in our walk with the Lord. Although we long for a
life that pleases God, the power of the flesh proves
too much for us and we fail.

Throughout the history of the church, men have
searched for ways to get the flesh under control. There
was a time when many Christians believed that the
only way to achieve victory was to lock themselves in

a closet at a monastery. They would deny themselves contact with anything or anyone who could possibly make them stumble. But even a casual look at the diaries they left behind shows that isolation didn't help.

Jerome, the famous theologian of the early church, lived for many years in a room that amounted to little more than a cage. His only contact with the outside world was a tiny window through which he would receive his meals. He closed himself off from everything and everybody in order that he might give himself totally to the study of God's Word, meditation, and prayer. But his personal journals record that the strictness of his lifestyle and the thickness of the surrounding walls didn't keep a barrage of horrible thoughts, imaginations, and fantasies away from his mind as he sat in his dark little cubicle.

Our help doesn't come until we realize the answer is far beyond our own resources. Crying out to God is the secret to our deliverance.

The flesh is a terribly strong enemy. Some Christians fight a losing battle with the flesh their entire walk with the Lord. They feel like the Israelites, who perished in the wilderness without ever entering into God's rest.

Why do such believers never enjoy God's victory? It's simple: they spend all their effort and energy trying to live a godly life in their own strength. Instead of turning their lives and struggles over to God, they keep searching for some new technique, some new method, some new program for righteousness. And none of them ever work.

As long as any of us try to deliver ourselves from "the body of this death" by desperately searching for another program or a formula to guide our efforts, we will fail. Our help doesn't come until we realize the answer is far beyond our own resources. Amazingly, crying out to God in weakness is the secret to our deliverance.

Not Another Self-Improvement Program

Our total powerlessness is a difficult thing for most of us to admit. We like to think of ourselves as strong, capable people, able to handle our own affairs. How many times have we started some self-improvement program, convinced that if we would just set our minds to it, we could easily lose a few pounds or get back in shape or eliminate a bothersome habit? But the sad fact is that as long as we think we can change our own lives by our own power, we never will.

One of the greatest barriers to growth in the Christian life is the notion that we can live a life that pleases God by our own efforts. If we think we can do this, we will try to take credit for it. "See, putting away that bad habit wasn't so hard! I knew I could do it!" At that point we are not giving God glory, but writing a success story with ourselves as the star. We begin telling others how our formula will work for them as well, and God becomes further and further removed from the picture. Predictably, despite our great self-confidence, the first wind of tragedy or disappointment causes our whole house of cards to come crashing down around our ears.

God will allow us to follow these self-help, self-improvement programs until we have tried them all. He will allow us to play out our own efforts until we finally come to the honest confession, "I can't do it. I can't be righteous in my own strength. Oh, wretched man that I am!" Such honesty is extremely difficult for us because it forces us to admit our own inability, failure, and weakness. We hate to come to these conclusions because they repudiate our pride.

It is only when we admit our utter powerlessness, however, that we find hope. When we finally turn to the grace of God, the Lord intervenes and begins to do a work that we could not do for ourselves. It is not until we find ourselves driven by desperation to a cry of helplessness and hopelessness that we begin to enjoy real victory in Christ.

The Struggle Begins

In one sense, the fact that a battle exists at all is a real cause for rejoicing. If we hadn't been made alive spiritually by God, there would be no conflict. If my spirit were still dead in trespasses and sins, I wouldn't be struggling with evil desires. I would dive right in and live after the flesh. The fact that we find ourselves in this fight is strong proof that we are indeed children of God.

And we *are* in a fight. Who can deny there is a ferocious battle going on inside each of us? In Galatians 5:17 the apostle Paul tells us, "For the flesh lusteth against the Spirit, and the Spirit against the flesh: and these are contrary the one to the other: so that ye cannot do the things that ye would."

Peter knew all about this struggle. At one time the burly fisherman boasted to Jesus that even if all the other disciples fled, he would not. Yet before the night was out he denied his Lord three times. Jesus had been right all along: the spirit is willing, but the flesh is weak.

Like Peter, we oftentimes react impulsively before we can get a grip on ourselves. We want to do right but find ourselves doing wrong. As Paul wrote, "I find then a law, that, when I would do good, evil is present with me. For I delight in the law of God after the inward man: But I see another law in my members, warring against the law of my mind, and bringing me into captivity to the law of sin which is in my members" (Romans 7:21-23).

We cannot know God's victory until we realize a war for control is constantly being waged within our members between the Holy Spirit and our flesh. Our flesh is not yet dead. Although we began to taste and enjoy the benefits of the Spirit when we committed our lives to Christ and although the fleshly nature was taken off the throne of our lives, the battle is not yet over. Before our conversion the flesh enjoyed dominating and controlling our lives, and until our bodies are redeemed, it will never give up its struggle to bring us back under its power.

Are Our Desires Wrong?

It is important at this point that we not make the mistake of thinking that our bodily drives and appetites themselves are evil. Our bodily desires were created by God and are absolutely necessary for sustaining life.

The strongest of all fleshly desires is our drive for air. There is nothing wrong with breathing, but it is possible to twist this natural function and use it to inhale cocaine. In so doing we take a natural, God-given function and pervert it to an unnatural end. The Bible calls that "sin."

Second only to the drive for air is our body's craving for moisture. There is nothing at all wrong with thirst, until we decide to quench it by sitting in a bar throwing down drinks until we can barely see straight. Again, we take a natural drive and use it for a purpose other than that for which God intended.

Our next strongest drive is hunger. There is nothing ungodly about eating, until we become so consumed with food that it begins to affect our health. Normally we associate an abuse of our natural desire for food with gluttony, yet equally harmful is the obsession some have with being thin. They live to count calories and compulsively exercise themselves into the ground. This, too, is sin.

The sex drive was created by God not only for procreation but also as a beautiful expression of mutual love between a husband and wife. But when we take this drive and make a pleasure toy out of it, love is no longer the focus and it becomes wrong.

Do you see how the twisting of all these beautiful, God-given drives for selfish gain becomes a thing that wars against the Spirit? All these bodily appetites were given to us by God, but He never intended that any of them should rule over us. They are a necessary part of life, but He did not design for them to dominate our lives.

Jesus said that if all we think about is what we're going to eat, drink, or wear, then there is no difference between ourselves and pagans (*see* Matthew 6:31,32). A person who doesn't know God can do nothing other than pursue bodily drives, but we believers know that life is more than food and the body more than clothes. The desires of our flesh are proper and right in their place, but were never intended by God to rule over us. Yet in our fallen state, the bodily appetites *do* seek to rule our lives. This is where the struggle begins.

The Master's Battle Plan

At this point the question arises, So, then, what are we to do with the flesh? God *has* made a provision for the flesh. He calls it "the cross."

Don't try to redeem the flesh or dress it up in spiritual trappings or reform it. It is not redeemable. It must be crucified. Paul stated, "Knowing this, that our old man [the old nature dominated by the flesh] is crucified with him, that the body of sin [our fallen nature that wants to rule] might be destroyed, that henceforth we should not serve sin" (Romans 6:6).

The biblical prescription for resolving the conflict between flesh and Spirit is not personal discipline or self-control. It is the power of the Holy Spirit.

Our job is to recognize this as truth. If the desires of the flesh were not still a factor in our lives, we would have no need to reckon that the old nature died with Christ. Whenever we encounter an area of the flesh that still controls us, we need to honestly acknowledge that the battle of the flesh and the Spirit remains in us. We need then to bring the specific area of weakness to the cross and reckon it crucified.

Yet that's only the first step! The biblical prescription for resolving the conflict between flesh and Spirit is not personal discipline or self-control. Power over the flesh comes only through a Spirit-controlled life. Although the conflict will be with us for as long as we live in these bodies, God provides us with the resources for spiritual victory. When we allow the Spirit of God to take over and work strongly in our lives, we can triumph over our fallen nature.

Any endeavor at sanctification attempted on our own is by definition a fleshly effort. When Paul was brought to the point of desperation and cried out, "O wretched man that I am!" He did not ask, "How can I find a strategy to do better next time? How can I try harder so I get more satisfactory results?" Paul had already gone down that road to futility. He realized that the power to live a godly life did not reside in him. He saw he needed a Deliverer and thus he cried, "Who shall deliver me?"

When Jesus awakens our spirit, He also gives us a new set of desires. We begin to long for intimate fellowship with God, a deeper knowledge and comprehension of His Word, and closer communion with others who are alive in Christ Jesus. We no longer desire to live after the flesh because we have come to realize that the end of such things is frustration and death. Living for the flesh always compelled us to reach out for something more, something just beyond our grasp, something that would finally bring a sense of lasting satisfaction. Yet the promised fulfillment always eluded us.

As we live after the Spirit, however, we discover a peace the world can't understand. The endless struggle—the aching emptiness—is gone and we discover a wonderful sense of purpose and meaning. The flesh no longer has the allure it once did and the battle inside us is won.

Spiritual Mind Games

Whether we like it or not, whether we admit it or not, there is a kind of perverse law at work within us that whenever we would do good, evil is present within. Paul accurately describes the often bewildering conflict that is so much a part of our lives: "For that which I do I allow not: for what I would, that do I not; but what I hate, that do I. If then I do that which I would not, I consent unto the law that it is good. Now then it is no more I that do it, but sin that dwelleth in me" (Romans 7:15-17).

Consider how we deal with one of the simplest, most direct commands in Scripture. Jesus said in John 13:34, "A new commandment I give unto you, That ye love one another." John later tells us that if we say we love God and yet hate our brother, we are liars (1 John 4:20). If we can't love our neighbor whom we have seen, John wonders, how can we love God whom we have not seen?

Enter our problem: Since the Bible so clearly forbids out-and-out hatred of a person, sometimes we try to soften the issue by saying, "Well, I don't hate him, I just hate the nasty things he does." But if we are honest, we must admit it is awfully hard to separate an individual from his actions. I, for one, have a difficult time making such a fine distinction. I find myself not only hating what a wicked man does, but him as well. If I hear that something unpleasant happened to him—like smashing up his new car in a traffic accident—I find myself inwardly rejoicing. I know the Bible says my attitude should be different, but it honestly isn't.

Oftentimes we end up playing mind games to convince ourselves that we are really obeying God and loving those who are unlovely. If we try hard enough, we can convince ourselves that we really do love and forgive. Yet the truth of our inward state becomes clear when that difficult person comes around, slaps us on the back, and with a loud voice announces to the entire room, "Gee, brother, I guess you didn't have time to use your deodorant this morning!" Our first reaction is to think, *You idiot! Now everyone is turning around and staring at me. Why don't you just drop dead, creep!* We really want to love this person, but our flesh won't allow us to!

Like Paul, we find an ironic law at work within us. Whenever we want to do good, evil is present. We end up getting frustrated with ourselves, sick of our failures, and overwhelmed with discouragement. We feel a profound sense of spiritual defeat and along with Paul cry out, "O wretched man that I am! Who shall deliver me from the body of this death?"

No Cause to Boast

Only when we admit that we are incapable of delivering ourselves from the law of sin and death can the doors be opened for the glorious power of God to work within us and do for us what we are incapable of doing for ourselves. As the power of God transforms us from the inside out, all we can do is give thanks and glory to God. We are unable to say to others, "I used to be involved with sin. But one day, I determined that Jesus didn't like it, so I mustered up my willpower and discipline and decided I just wouldn't do those things anymore." There is no room for boasting about what fine, self-controlled people we are. As the Scriptures declare, "God forbid that I should glory, save in the cross of our Lord Jesus Christ" (Galatians 6:14).

Have you ever run into people who seemed more spiritual than they actually were? A dead giveaway of this kind of insincerity comes when someone speaks of a spiritual struggle. If a person admits having a battle with the flesh, these "spiritual" people immediately put a self-righteous, holier-than-thou expression on their faces. Without saying a word, they communicate that fighting with the flesh is some terrible abnormality for a believer. "Why, if you just prayed more, and spent more time in the Word, and were spiritually minded (like us), you wouldn't have any problem with your flesh."

While such attitudes of superspiritual perfectionism are very common, they don't line up with the clear teaching of Scripture. I don't believe we will ever experience a time, while we live here on earth, when we won't have a problem with these fleshly bodies. I know through long experience that my own flesh can be just as troublesome as it ever was.

When God reveals to me an area of the flesh He wants to change, for example, I always start out with the best of intentions. I see the ugliness of my sin and vow that I will never fall in that manner again. And so I come up with various disciplines and strategies to deal with the problem. I seek out all kinds of advice on how to practically deal with the situation. But sooner or later I watch all my best-laid plans fall apart. I get so frustrated that I cry out, "God, help me!" And then amazingly enough, He does. His Spirit miraculously begins to transform my life.

As I overflow with gratitude, I see how God's way of transformation is so wonderfully simple and yet much better than my own misguided efforts. I find myself shaking my head and saying, "When will I ever understand this simple concept of grace?" How could I ever imagine that, somewhere down the line, I could do something worthwhile and prove to God that I'm not a total wretch? Yet I do imagine it.

God never intended that the flesh rule over us, and He has provided the resources and the power for us to experience victory. But as long as we are committed to trying to work out our own struggles, even our best efforts get in the way. Any attempt at godliness that arises from our own strength is a work of the flesh and is just as detestable in God's sight as the thing we are trying not to do. When our victory comes from God's intervention alone, outside of our own resources, the end result is glory and praise unto God.

A Trap to Avoid

In those moments when we feel close to the Lord, it is tempting to say, "This is so beautiful, I am never going to live after the flesh again, for that is so pointless and empty!" Unfortunately, however, tomorrow comes and we forget all about our good intentions. As we drag ourselves to bed at the end of a long and frustrating day, it suddenly dawns on us that despite our best efforts, we wandered away, did our own thing, and were controlled by the flesh. Much to our surprise, our flesh grabbed the reins once more and we found ourselves doing what we promised we would never do again.

It is at that moment that we often make our biggest mistake. We begin blaming and condemning ourselves and vow that we are going to try harder next time. Do you see the problem? As soon as we make such promises, we have decided to invest confidence in our flesh. We are saying that our own efforts will make us spiritually strong and we have stepped back into the realm of the flesh. Like Peter, we are saying, "I will never deny you!"

Many of us grow intensely frustrated when it seems we are continually fighting the same battles over and over. Yet this shouldn't surprise us. All of us go through a predictable set of steps in which we first must come to the end of our rope and realize that in our own strength we can't live in a way that pleases God. We cry out to God in desperation, and He works His gracious deliverance. I would like to think that there is some way in which I might not have to hit bottom so regularly; but unfortunately, I have yet to discover it.

From the Inside Out

In His grace, God has made it possible for us to enjoy consistent victory. Still, this side of heaven, the battle never ends. Each day presents the choice we each must make. Will we live for the desires of the flesh, or will we yield our lives to the transforming power of the Spirit of God?

How glorious it is to come to the end of our resources and to see God change our lives by His grace! Our only boast as believers is in the finished work of Jesus Christ on our behalf. If it were not for the cross, we would all be hopelessly lost forever. But because of God's great love for us, we who were formerly lost have been saved and baptized into Christ.

We can now have such a wonderful relationship with God that it is no longer we who live, but Christ lives in us. The life we now live, we live by faith in the Son of God, who loved us and gave Himself for us. Because of God's grace, each of us are now a new creation in Christ Jesus. Old things are passed away; everything has become new.

When we become children of God, the spiritual side of us comes alive. We suddenly realize that there is more to life than obeying the instincts of the flesh. We come to understand that the inner hunger which our flesh could never satisfy can be fulfilled in a loving relationship with God. The more we come to know God, the more we experience His peace and joy and discover that the level of satisfaction we encounter in the Spirit is limitlessly beyond the narrow spectrum of the flesh.

How beautiful it is when we let go of our own futile efforts and allow the Spirit to work! For His victory comes from the inside out, not the outside in. And that's the kind of victory that *lasts*.

Grace

Free Indeed!

N O ONE IN THE world is truly as free as a
believer in Jesus Christ. As Paul said in Galatians 5:1, "Stand fast therefore in the liberty wherewith Christ hath made us free, and be not entangled
again with the yoke of bondage."

Freedom means a state of free moral agency—the
capacity to make real choices in life. While believers
are truly free, it is wrong to use that term to describe
a sinner. The sinner has only one true choice—whether
to put his or her faith in Jesus. He is in such bondage
to his flesh that he cannot stop what he is doing.

Many people today do evil things without knowing why they do them. They say, "I hate it; I don't
want to do it; I don't understand why I do it. I hate
myself for doing it, but I do it anyway." They are
bound and held by a power—the power of Satan.

Before we came to Christ, all of us were children of wrath and our whole manner of life was spent trying to fulfill the desires of the flesh and mind *(see* Ephesians 2:3). Our only option was which manner of bondage we would choose. We weren't free moral agents because we had no capacity to turn from sin. We might exchange one form of ungodliness for another, but we were incapable of living righteously. There is no freedom to be found in such a dreadful condition.

To remain free, we must not exercise our liberty in any area that will bring us back under bondage.

What a contrast to the glorious liberty we have been given in Christ Jesus! As recipients of God's love and forgiveness, we have been granted freedom from the domination of our flesh. We no longer have to live as slaves to our own fleshly desires. We have been granted the capacity to turn from sin to serve and worship God. We have been set free from the chains of darkness that held us in bondage. Through our believing and trusting in Jesus Christ, we are free from having to live according to a standard of the law in order to be accepted by God. As children of God, we have a taste of liberty and freedom like nothing we have ever known.

We are free in Christ, and the extent of our liberty is so vast that Paul could say, "All things are lawful for me" (1 Corinthians 10:23). There is no broader ethic contained in any philosophy in the world. In fact, the man who can say, "All things are lawful for me" is the freest man who ever lived.

But Paul also insisted that while all things are lawful for us, "all things are not expedient" (verse 23). That is, although there are areas of freedom we could pursue that wouldn't put our salvation in jeopardy, they would impede our progress in our walk with God. We are to avoid areas that would distract us from a simple, wholehearted devotion to God. If we are to remain free, we must be careful not to exercise our liberty in any area that will bring us back under bondage.

Freedom Badly Used

So many times people misunderstand Christian liberty, thinking that freedom in Christ means they can freely commit all kinds of sin. They use their freedom as an occasion for the flesh. This is a total perversion of what Scripture teaches about Christian liberty. Our liberty is never a freedom to sin freely; it is never a license to sin.

The glorious liberty we have been called to in Christ Jesus is first of all a freedom from our flesh and the domination that our flesh once held over us. In Romans 6, Paul tells us this freedom in Christ is a freedom to serve and worship God. We are free *not* to live the sinful, sensual kind of life that we once lived.

In Eden, Adam was granted tremendous freedom. He could eat from any tree in the garden except the tree of the knowledge of good and evil. God knew from the beginning that Adam would disobey His command, eat from the forbidden tree, and thus bring sin and misery into the world. Even so, God did not physically prevent Adam from eating the fruit. Adam misused his freedom and we suffer the catastrophic consequences of his choice today. Sin came into the world through one man's wrong exercise of freedom.

In like manner, we can choose to make wrong use of our freedom in Christ. It is possible for us to take this glorious freedom and exercise it in such a way that we are brought back into bondage. We have all heard people say things like, "Well, as a Christian I am free. Thus I intend to gratify this impulse of my flesh because I have freedom to do so." We must remember that we also have freedom *not* to do so. We should never use our freedom as an occasion for our flesh—to yield to its impulses. Hebrews 12:1,2 tells us to "lay aside every weight, and the sin which doth so easily beset us," and to "run with patience the race that is set before us, looking unto Jesus the author and finisher of our faith."

Freedom to Serve

It's clear how we should *not* use our freedom in Christ. The real question is, How *should* we use it? How can we use our freedom in a way that honors God and helps us to grow in grace? Paul had the answer in Galatians 5:13. He said we should use our freedom to serve one another in love: "For, brethren, ye have been called unto liberty; only use not liberty for an occasion to the flesh, but by love serve one another." Scripture constantly reminds us of the high value God places on humble servitude.

Over and over, the Bible reminds us that if we want to be really great in God's kingdom, we must serve. Jesus made a magnificent statement to His disciples at the beginning of what we call the Great Commission. He said, "All power is given unto me in heaven and in earth" (Matthew 28:18). Can you imagine how much power that must be? *All* the power of the universe was given to Him. The same power that lit the fires of the stars and holds every atom together belongs to Jesus.

And what did He do with this power? Shake the universe? Spin out a few new galaxies? No. Jesus took off His robe, girded Himself about as a servant, and washed His disciples' feet. After He had washed the last dirty ankles and toes, He asked His men, in effect, "Do you know what I have done? I have given you an example. For if I, being your Lord, have served you, then so also ought you to serve one another" (*see* John 13:12-14).

What if right now you could say, "All power in the universe is mine"? What would you do with such power? Jesus took a towel and a basin of water and washed the filthy feet of His disciples. All power in the universe was His—and what did He do with it? He washed the disciples' feet.

There are very few of us who want to serve. Instead, we love to give orders and be waited on. "Go get me that!" "Hand that tool to me." "I need you to go." How we love to give orders, and how we get upset when the orders aren't fulfilled! We get hurt, we pout. We enjoy being part of the ruling class . . . but God's greatest blessings are not to be found there. We have been set free not to boss others around, but to serve one another in love.

Without question, this blessing requires a work of God's Spirit within our hearts. My flesh certainly rebels at the idea of serving someone else in love. Often my immediate reaction to even the simplest request is, "If you want a glass of water, go get it yourself. Who was your slave yesterday?" My flesh loves to be catered to. It clamors to be served. But I have been set free from bondage to my flesh and now I can serve others in love. What a joy it is to serve in love! All of the law is encapsulated in one phrase: "Thou shalt love thy neighbour as thyself" (Matthew 22:39).

Freedom to Love

Two hundred years before Jesus, Buddha said, "Don't do to others what you don't want them to do to you." Notice he put it in the negative. If you don't want someone to bust you in the nose, then don't bust him in the nose. It is a negative injunction.

The golden rule isn't merely avoiding wrong; it's actively seeking out practical ways to express love.

There are a lot of people around today who mistake Buddha's advice for the golden rule. They believe they are righteous because of what they *don't* do. "Well," they may say, "I don't hurt anybody. I've never killed anyone and I don't sleep around." Their lives becomes so predicated on negatives that they literally become "good for nothing."

But observe that Jesus framed this ethic in distinctly positive terms. He said, "As ye would that men should do to you, do ye also to them likewise" (Luke 6:31). Even as I would like to be served, I should serve. Even as I would like to be loved, I should love. Even as I would like to receive gifts, I should give.

Loving our neighbors as ourselves means taking the initiative to do for others in a creative, active, and joyful manner. The golden rule isn't merely about avoiding wrong, but rather, it's about actively seeking out practical ways to express our love.

Jesus says we fulfill the law first by loving God then by loving others and treating them as we would like to be treated. We like others to speak well of us, so we should speak well of them. We like others to overlook our faults, so we should extend the same gracious attitude toward them.

Churchgoing Cannibalism

Why is it that when someone says something unkind about us, often our first response is to take them down a few pegs? We drop a few remarks to the effect that our critics aren't quite as holy as they'd like others to think. "Well, I only like to speak the truth, and I want to tell you about him," we say. Then when they hear what we have been saying, another round is triggered in an endless cycle of backbiting and ill will.

On the other hand, if I find out someone really likes me and is saying nice things about me, I say, "Well, he is surely an excellent judge of character. He is just a marvelous person, you know."

It used to be that when someone was intent on tearing another person to pieces, I would bait him on. After he had dumped his load of garbage I would say, "Well, that is very interesting. I guess you didn't know he was my uncle, did you?" I liked to watch the reaction.

Paul warned us, "If ye bite and devour one another, take heed that ye be not consumed one of another" (Galatians 5:15). If we find ourselves in the practice of biting and devouring one another—speaking cutting, destructive, even sarcastic words about one another—we are walking in the antithesis of love. Sadly, a kind of interpersonal, relational cannibalism begins to take place. We find ourselves trapped in a destructive, vicious circle. Jealousy and bitterness and striving develop and soon the church is eating itself up. We are being consumed one of another.

I once read an account of a man in England who successfully bred a particularly vicious breed of game cocks. His roosters were almost invincible in the pit, and the man took great pride in the stature and reputation he had gained as a result of his efforts. Each morning he would walk out and admire his fighting birds.

One day he went out to inspect his roosters and, much to his horror, found their pen littered with feathers, blood, and carcasses. His precious stock was lying about, ripped to shreds. He quickly called one of his hired hands and asked what had happened. "Who was so stupid as to put these aggressive creatures in the same pen?" he thundered. The servant replied meekly, "I did, sir." "And why would you do such a stupid thing?" demanded the owner. "Well," said the employee, "I figured by now they would all know they are fighting on the same side." But of course, the birds were too stupid to recognize the real enemy.

Unfortunately, there are times when we in the church hardly perform on a more intelligent level. We often forget who our real enemy is. The enemy is not a group of Baptists or Presbyterians. Our real enemy is the power of darkness that holds men in slavery to deception and sin. We need to quit our self-destructive rivalries and begin working together for the common good of God's kingdom. For if we bite and devour one another, we are going to be consumed by one another. One day we are going to find the church bloody and broken and the world will say, "Look—that's Christianity for you!"

How tragic that so much of the history of the church has been spent in devouring and consuming one another. We are far too given to unfairly labeling and putting down those in other fellowships, and nothing could be more counterproductive to the progress of the kingdom of God.

As free men and women in Christ, we need to walk in the Spirit—the Spirit of love, forgiveness, and kindness. We must look to the Lord for His grace and empowerment. This is not an elective for us. Where else will we find the strength to run against this destructive tide and focus on what is good and praiseworthy in others, even those with whom we disagree?

The Responsibility of Freedom

With freedom comes great responsibility. *Always.* The price of freedom is eternal vigilance, someone once said. We must be on guard to maintain our freedom because it is terribly easy to lose.

Do not be misled into misusing your freedom to gratify your flesh. Yes, we are free in Christ to act as we choose. And yes, while God may not condemn your soul to hell over some questionable activity, ask yourself: Does it slow you down? Is it impeding your progress toward the goal?

The main goal and desire of my life is to be found in Christ, complete in Him. Paul said, "Know ye not that they which run in a race run all, but one

receiveth the prize? So run, that ye may obtain"
(1 Corinthians 9:24). I intend to "press toward the
mark for the prize of the high calling of God in Christ
Jesus" (Philippians 3:14). "Wherefore . . . let us lay
aside every weight, and the sin which doth so easily
beset us, and let us run with patience the race that is
set before us, looking unto Jesus the author and finisher of our faith" (Hebrews 12:1,2).

I don't want anything to slow me down. I don't
want anything to impede my progress. Someone
might tell me, "But Chuck, there is nothing wrong
with X. A Christian can do that." Sure he can. But it
can also impede his progress toward the goal! "All
things are lawful unto me, but all things are not
expedient" (1 Corinthians 6:12). Some lawful things
tear me down and harm my relationship with
Jesus. "All things are lawful for me, but I will not be
brought under the power of any" (verse 12).

If I am to remain free, I must be careful not to
exercise my freedom in pursuing anything that could
bring me under its power. Once I have succumbed to
its power, I am no longer free. If I want to exercise
my freedom in activities that get a grip on me and
will not let me go, then I am no longer free. I have
been foolish in the exercise of my freedom and have
brought myself back into bondage. And that's no way
to live.

Thank God, we have been given freedom in
Christ! Thank God, we have been given the resources
to maintain that freedom! Mere words cannot
express what it means to be truly *free*.

May the Lord help us to freely love, to freely
serve, to freely seek the best interests of one another.
For then, at last, we shall be capable of fully enjoying
the incomparable delights to be found only in the
freedom of God's great grace.

10
Grace

Won't They
Go Wild?

MANY PEOPLE HAVE A great, unfounded
fear that the grace of God will lead to sinful
living. They fear that if believers realize God doesn't
judge them by works but by faith in Christ, they will
run wild. "Wait a minute, Chuck!" they say. "You
open the door like this and people are going to do all
kinds of evil or horrible things and rationalize it by
saying, 'His grace covers everything I do.'"

This objection is not new. Paul's preaching of the
gospel of grace among the Gentiles brought immediate protests from the Jews. They thought that given
such liberty, the Gentiles would go crazy. Peter, too,
could see the dangers of misinterpreting Paul's gospel, and in his epistle said, "As our beloved brother
Paul also according to the wisdom given unto him
hath written unto you; as also in all his epistles,

speaking in them of these things; in which are some things hard to be understood, *which they that are unlearned and unstable wrest, as they do also the other scriptures, unto their own destruction*" (2 Peter 3:15,16).

Unfortunately, there always have been those who take the Word of God and twist it from its context—to their own destruction. They take Paul's gospel as an excuse for a riotous life of sin. But the gospel can never be truly understood in that way.

You're Dead!

In Romans 5, Paul lays out our relationship with God through grace in strong, glorious terms. In verse 20 he states, "Where sin abounded, grace did much more abound." In the first verse of the next chapter he imagines some people saying, "Well, then, let's go out and do a lot of sinning so that grace might much more abound. The abounding grace of God is wonderful. Let's give it a chance to *really* abound." Paul answers, in effect, "Perish the thought! How can we who are dead to sin live any longer therein?" (*see* Romans 6:2). His answer contains an important key to the Christian walk and experience.

Suppose I was caught robbing a bank. I am sent to jail and am put on trial. After many weeks, the jury comes in with a verdict: "We find him guilty." The judge then appoints the day when I am to be sentenced. I am looking at five to life because I used a gun and shot holes in the ceiling and scared the tellers silly. Finally, the day arrives that I am to appear before the judge for sentencing.

The law has done its job. It has apprehended and condemned the guilty. I go into court and the judge says, "Will the defendant please rise." I stand up, and he says, "The court finds you guilty and you are sentenced to spend five years to life in the state penitentiary." The news is so bad that I have a heart attack and die right on the spot.

Does the court keep my carcass in jail for five years? No. My death immediately sets me free from the condemnation of the law. My sentence has no more power over me because I am a dead man.

This is the point Paul makes about those of us who, through faith in Jesus Christ, have been justified before God and are now living under His glorious grace. We are no longer living after the flesh; our old self is dead. The law had sentenced us to death. The demands of the law were fulfilled when we became crucified with Christ. The old me and you were crucified. So if the old self is dead, then how can we be living any longer in sin? We are dead to that old life.

"I am crucified with Christ," writes Paul, "nevertheless I live; yet not I, but Christ liveth in me" (Galatians 2:20). We don't live an old, selfish life anymore. Our ego-centered days are over. No longer do we live after the flesh. We are now free from the law, our sinful nature, and our awful guilt because our old, guilty man was crucified with Jesus Christ. Now we walk after God by trusting in Jesus.

If You're Dead, Act Like It

The kind of faith that brings me a righteous standing before God is the kind of faith that manifests itself in the works of God. If I am still living in the filth and corruption of my old flesh—using the grace of God as a cloak for my lascivious way of life—then I am only deceiving myself. I am not really a child of

God. James 2:26 says, "For as the body without the spirit is dead, so faith without works is dead also."

A person who has been born of the Spirit of God *will* manifest it in his lifestyle. Jesus said, "Why call ye me Lord, Lord, and do not the things which I say? Whosoever cometh to me, and heareth my sayings, and doeth them, I will shew you to whom he is like: He is like a man which built an house, and digged deep, and laid the foundation on a rock: and when the flood arose, the stream beat vehemently upon that house, and could not shake it: for it was founded upon a rock. But he that heareth, and doeth not, is like a man that without a foundation built an house upon the earth; against which the stream did beat vehemently, and immediately it fell; and the ruin of that house was great" (Luke 6:46-49).

The apostle John wrote, "And hereby we do know that we know him, if we keep his commandments. He that saith, I know him, and keepeth not his commandments, is a liar, and the truth is not in him" (1 John 2:3,4). And twice in that same letter he adds that whoever is born of God cannot practice sin (*see* 1 John 3:9; 5:18). Do not frustrate the grace of God. Believe and trust in Jesus Christ as your Lord and Savior and walk in the newness of that relationship.

Love God and Do What You Will

At this point, some will ask, "Still, if our good works don't save us, what's to keep us from running around smoking, or carousing, or hanging out in seedy bars?" It's not that I *can't* do these things; I simply don't have the desire. The love of Christ constrains me to live a life that pleases Him. Having tasted the goodness of His love, I don't want to walk away from Him. I want to draw as close to Jesus as possible because I love Him and He loves me. I don't want to get involved in anything that would dishonor Him.

Ironically, I live a much straighter life under grace than I ever did under the law. Under a legal relationship I am always pressing the limits. I am always trying to ascertain whether specific actions are right or wrong. I am always looking for loopholes. I rationalize and justify the things I am doing. I live to the legal limits, plus a little bit more.

God doesn't want to bind you with law; He wants to draw you to Himself with His love. This is the gospel of grace.

A love relationship with God is vastly different from that. No longer do I debate whether something is right or wrong. Rather, I find myself asking, "Is this pleasing to my Father? I love Him and want to please Him. He loves me so much that I don't want to hurt Him. Would my Father be pleased if I did this?" Sometimes even where the law is silent, my heart tells me God would be grieved if I carried out an activity I'm considering.

A loving relationship is what God is seeking with each of us. He doesn't want to bind you with a law. He wants to draw you with His love to Himself. This is the gospel of God's grace, the righteousness which God imputed to us apart from the law.

So many of us fail to understand that love is the only true motivation for goodness. Fear is never a primary, driving force in the Christian life. If we are good only because we are afraid to be bad, that is not true righteousness. We can have circumspect external conduct as a cover for all kinds of wrong and twisted motivations. If fear of consequences is the only thing that keeps us in check, we may merely be an example of evil under restraint. That isn't true goodness. True goodness is always and exclusively motivated by love. If our moral choices are based on fervent love and a desire to abstain from things that grieve the heart of God, we have discovered the true motive of righteousness.

The fruit of the Spirit is love. One of the outstanding characteristics of love is goodness. When we are conscious of love, we experience joy. When love takes hold of our lives, we know peace. The demonstration of love is always patience and long-suffering. The character of love is gentleness and kindness. The bottom line is that when the Spirit is producing His fruit in us, the need for burdensome externals like the law disappears. *The law is fulfilled by love.*

So we make a wonderful discovery: a righteous life is no longer a burden to us but a joy because we have a love relationship with Jesus.

A Lingering Problem

It is possible for us to know and experience the grace of God. We can live in the joy and peace of justification by faith in Jesus Christ and the confident assurance of our righteous standing before God in Him. This confidence comes through the knowledge that I was crucified with Christ. The life dominated by my flesh is dead and I now live a new life dominated by the Spirit of Jesus Christ. I have a new nature, the nature of Jesus Christ. "Therefore if any man be in Christ, he is a new creature: old things are passed away; behold, all things are become new" (2 Corinthians 5:17). This is an incredibly liberating truth.

But I still have a problem. I am still in this body, and as long as I am in this state I am subject to the powerful forces of my bodily drives. Thus, there is warfare going on inside of me. The flesh brings up his guns and begins to fire away. My flesh—my old man—is dead, and yet it's as if I have to carry this old carcass around with me. I'm like the partner of Sam McGee, living with "a corpse half hid that he couldn't get rid."

It's crucial to remember that Scripture makes an important distinction: My spirit is redeemed, but my body is not. That creates a tremendous conflict. Paul declared in Romans 8:22,23, "For we know that the whole creation groaneth and travaileth in pain together until now. And not only they, but ourselves also, which have the firstfruits of the Spirit, even we ourselves groan within ourselves, waiting for the adoption, [that is,] the redemption of our body." How often I groan and weep before God because of the weaknesses of my flesh.

After Jesus had prayed in the garden of Gethsemane, He came to the disciples and found them asleep. He said to Peter, "Simon, sleepest thou? Couldst not thou watch one hour? Watch ye and pray, lest ye enter into temptation. The spirit truly is ready, but the flesh is weak" (Mark 14:37,38). No truer words were ever spoken. My spirit, indeed, is willing, but my flesh is weak. I groan and travail and I say, "Oh God, hasten the day when you deliver me from this body of corruption!" I am anxious to get rid of this old corpse.

*In my moment of
weakness, the Spirit raises
up conviction and power
and my mind is turned
toward the Lord.*

One day, we will all be liberated from our fallen nature. Scripture says, "For this corruptible must put on incorruption, and this mortal must put on immortality. So when this corruptible shall have put on incorruption, and this mortal shall have put on immortality, then shall be brought to pass the saying that is written, Death is swallowed up in victory. O death, where is thy sting? O grave, where is thy victory? The sting of death is sin; and the strength of sin is the law. But thanks be to God, which giveth us the victory through our Lord Jesus Christ" (1 Corinthians 15:53-57).

In the meantime, all is not lost. In my moment of weakness, the Spirit raises up conviction and power and my mind is turned toward the Lord. I seek His help and His strength. I begin to experience His victory. I have found that I must rely *daily* upon the strength and power of Jesus Christ to live the life He wants me to live. There is no place where I can put my life in neutral and coast along. The minute I do, the flesh begins to rise up and usurp power and authority. I must keep my appetites subdued, or else they will rule over me. Paul wrote, "I keep under my body, and bring it into subjection: lest that by any means, when I have preached to others, I myself should be a castaway [or disapproved]" (1 Corinthians 9:27).

Now, if I am caught off guard and find myself again yielding to the flesh, does that mean I am no longer saved? Do I have to get saved all over again? No. I still believe in Jesus Christ. I still love the Lord and it is still my faith that is imputed to me for righteousness. It is precisely because of my faith and my new life in Christ that I cannot go on being dominated by my flesh.

Though I may fall into a pit for a time, I can't stay there. God won't let me stay in that state. He won't let me get by with some of the things that I might like to do that everybody else is doing. They may do it and get by with it, but I won't. He will see to it that I won't! If I try to follow worldly ways and do the things that the "life in the fast lane" crowd does, I am either going to fail at it, hate it, or get caught. Because He loves us and we are His children, we simply can't get by with sin like the world does.

Are There No Standards at All?

Someone may still be wondering, *So if we are under grace, can we simply ignore God's standards of personal conduct?* Not at all. In our new relationship, we have received the dynamic of God's power and the indwelling presence of the Holy Spirit. In Christ we receive a new nature that longs to live in harmony with God's love and holiness. Through the power of the Holy Spirit we need no longer strain and strive to do what is right. This is what John meant when he wrote, "This is love for God: to obey his commands. And his commands are not burdensome" (1 John 5:3, NIV). God's presence within us empowers us to choose what is right and to refrain from evil.

Those who have read the classics are probably familiar with the story of Ulysses. During his travels, this ancient adventurer heard stories of the island of the sirens—deadly enchantresses who made such beautiful music that any sailors passing by would turn their ships toward shore and be dashed upon the rocks. No one had ever heard the song of these sirens and lived. This sounded like a worthy challenge to a daring man like Ulysses. He decided to become the first to hear this music and survive.

In order to achieve his goal, Ulysses put wax in the ears of his crew and instructed his men to tie him securely to the ship's mast. As they rowed past the island of the sirens, the seductive music began. Ulysses began to strain against the ropes, struggling to get loose so he could swim to shore. He cursed at his sailors to turn the boat toward the rocks, but the wax prevented them from hearing his cries. Ulysses continued to fight against his bonds until the ship moved out of range and into safety. Ulysses had heard the song of the sirens and lived—yet ever after he was haunted by the memory of the beguiling music.

Greek myths also tell of another ship that passed this island and yet survived. As its crew was being drawn by the deadly melody to disaster on the shoals, a gifted man on board named Orpheus grabbed a lyre and began to play. The music of Orpheus so far surpassed that of the sirens that the men turned away from the rocks and sailed to safety, enraptured by these new, exquisite melodies that gave life.

When we face the pull of temptation, most of us can relate to either Ulysses or Orpheus. For some, the siren song of the world has an almost irresistible attraction. They find themselves bound in place by the law, yet struggling against the rules when enticed by the power of the flesh. Their only hope is in the law that holds them back.

The joy of oneness in Christ far surpasses anything the world or the flesh can offer.

But there are those who have heard a new song—the music of heaven in their hearts. They discover that the love of Jesus Christ is so strong and satisfying that, although the world is still attractive, they gladly leave it behind so they may be powerfully drawn into His beautiful presence. They don't have to be tied or bound. They aren't struggling against restricting ropes. They have discovered the glory of walking with God in intimate fellowship.

The joy of such oneness in Christ far surpasses anything the world or the flesh can offer. The allure and attraction of sin has lost its power. Those who have discovered this kind of fulfillment don't need laws. Instead of slavishly following a regulation that says, "Now, don't bash your neighbor's head in!" they have no desire to do so because their heart has been touched by the love of God. They simply want to see their neighbor saved.

Just the other day, I saw this principle in action. As I was driving down a busy street near Calvary Chapel a car pulled in front of me, causing me to nearly lock up my breaks. The car was driven by a little, gray-haired old lady. She didn't see me or a number of others she nearly ran into. If the other drivers had not paid close attention, there would have been a terrible accident. She made so many foolish moves I found myself praying, "Lord, please help that little old lady get home safely." Those who know me will testify that my attitude of concern in that situation was nothing short of a miracle! It is glorious to be able to experience the changes brought about by our loving relationship with God through Jesus Christ.

A Constant Love

Because of Christ, we can experience true oneness with God. God isn't close to us one moment and distant the next. And even if we fail, even though we are still weak in so many areas, our righteous standing before God doesn't vary with our shifting attitudes or changing moods. Our relationship with God is steady and secure because it isn't based upon us or our performance. Our relationship is predicated upon the work of Jesus Christ on our behalf. He took our sins upon Himself and died in our place to make our salvation by faith a reality. We can leave behind the mentality that says God only loves us when we are "good" and rejects us when we are bad.

I call my granddaughter on the phone quite often. I like to talk to her in the morning and ask her how things are going. Sometimes when I talk to her, she says, "I am a grouchy girl today, Grandpa." Do I love her less when she says that? She knows that she is out of sorts. But it doesn't alter my love for her one bit. Nor do I love her any more when she is a sweet little angel. I just love her. I love her grouchy and I love her sweet.

God looks at us the same way. When we are grouchy we are prone to think, *God can't love me today. I don't even love myself. I am miserable. I don't want anyone around me.* We are also prone to think God doesn't love us when we have failed. Not so! If our standing before God were based on our performance, it never would have been necessary for Jesus Christ to die.

When Jesus accounts our faith as righteousness, He gives us a beautiful, stable, loving relationship with Himself. We enjoy the kind of standing that says, "Come on in and sit down. Let Me help you; let Me strengthen you."

God loves you. You are so very dear to Him that He chose you and called you to be His eternally. That is why the grace of God does not lead to wild living. There's infinitely more joy to be had in the Savior than in sin.

11
Grace

Booby Traps and Land Mines

I T SEEMS THERE ARE always those who stand
ready to move into harvested territory in order to
glean off some of the crop.

In Calvary Chapel's parking lot, we often catch
people distributing flyers which promote weird
doctrines. At other times we've seen people stand in
the driveway and try to put some kind of a doctrinal
trip on the parishioners as they are coming in. We
always ask, "Why would you go to a church to pass
out your flyers?" If we were holding some special
event and planned to pass out flyers to announce
it, we would send our kids to the beach or to the
shopping centers—not to another church! Why would
you go to a church to try to siphon off those who
already are established there?

If you have a vital doctrine that you feel others must understand and believe, then rather than trying to convert us, why not grant us the privilege of seeing how that truth has transformed *your* life into the image of Jesus Christ? Let us see that truth demonstrated in your own life. When we see your glorious commitment and your close walk with the Lord, we no doubt will ask you what is going on because you have something we need.

Sadly, people are never satisfied to do that. It is tragic that they feel they have a divine calling to rip off the body of Christ to another persuasion. That is why the New Testament is full of warnings and exhortations against false teachers and their cunning and charming ways.

You Can Be Sure

All cults tend to pervert the gospel of Christ. Usually they heavily emphasize works and a works-related righteousness. If you ask a person involved in one of these cults if they are born again, quite often they will respond, "Brother, you won't know that until you die, because you don't know what your last works are going to be." Now, wouldn't that be a horrible time to find out?

God wants us to have assurance of our salvation, and if we depend upon Jesus Christ and His work, we can have it. If our salvation is based upon works,

---

The Bible teaches that the way of salvation is indeed a narrow way.

---

then assurance is beyond our grasp. If our salvation is based upon faithfulness to a creed or to a system of works, then we won't know our eternal destiny until we die . . . and then it will be too late. But if our salvation is based upon faith in Jesus Christ and His work alone, we can be sure.

You know, I am not sure of my works. I am not sure of my self-righteousness. I *am* sure of His work and His righteousness. As the hymnwriter put it, "My hope is built on nothing less, than Jesus' blood and righteousness; I dare not trust the sweetest frame, but wholly lean on Jesus' name." Paul is so convinced of this truth that he writes, "Though we, or an angel from heaven, preach any other gospel unto you than that which we have preached unto you, let him be accursed" (Galatians 1:8). Strong words! Paul uses the term *anathema*, which means "cursed to the lowest hell."

Suppose that some angel sits on your bed tonight. You feel restless, wake up, and see a glowing creature sitting there on the foot of your bed, seven feet tall. If he says, "Don't be afraid! I have come to share some good news with you. You are a special person—God has chosen you for a special work. If you will just get in and do this work for God, He will save you." What should you conclude? One thing is for sure: This angel is not from God. Let him be accursed.

The Bible teaches that the way of salvation is indeed a narrow way. Paul's words strike a death blow to the broad kind of religion so popular today that says, "I believe a person who is doing what he feels is right in his own heart will be accepted by God." Peter said, "[Christ] is the stone which was set at nought of you builders, which is become the head of the corner [that is, chief cornerstone]. Neither is there salvation in any other: for there is none other name under heaven given among men, whereby we must be saved" (Acts 4:11,12).

Many people today would respond, "Oh Peter, you are too narrow. You mean to tell me that Jesus is the only way? That is too narrow, Peter. I can't follow that." Very well. Then be accursed. "But those are such harsh words," they reply. "That is too narrow. Surely, Jesus was broader than that!" But it was Jesus Himself who said, "I am the way, the truth and the life: no man cometh unto the Father, but by me" (John 14:6). And it was Jesus who said, "Enter ye in at the strait gate: for wide is the gate, and broad is the way, that leadeth to destruction, and many there be which go in thereat: because strait is the gate, and narrow is the way, which leadeth unto life, and few there be that find it" (Matthew 7:13,14).

Paul had it right all along. Even today you can almost hear him pleading with the Galatians: "Look, I am going to say it again. If I or an angel of heaven or any man come and lay on you any other trip—one that gets you to rely on yourself, in your own works, in your own goodness, in your own righteousness, in your keeping of the law, in your being circumcised, in your following some ritual, in your joining some group, in your giving so much—let him be accursed!"

Why was Paul so adamant? Because God has accepted us just as we are—as we put our faith in His Son Jesus Christ. By our trust in Him, He has cleansed us from all our sins and He has received us. God desires to bestow upon us the richness and the fullness of His love—not because we deserve it, but because He loves us. This is the gospel of grace in Jesus Christ. This is what Paul eventually died for.

It's a Marvel

Do you ever wonder why the doctrines that teach

good works as the basis for relating to God seem to gain such a strong foothold in people's lives? I confess I have.

No doubt Paul wondered too, for he said to the Galatians, "I marvel that ye are so soon removed from him that called you into the grace of Christ unto another gospel" (Galatians 1:6). It *is* a marvel that people would leave the grace of Christ for another gospel—especially when this "gospel" isn't good news at all!

Whenever a person says, "It's good to believe in Jesus Christ, but it takes more than that," watch out! The minute you tell me that I have to be righteous and must prove myself before God by my holiness, you are not bringing me to God; you are pushing me away from Him. I am not righteous and I am not holy and there is no way I can be, so what you are telling me is *not* good news. It is far from good news. It's a proclamation of death.

Paul could not understand why anyone would want to leave a loving relationship with God to try to establish a relationship based on works, circumcision, or through keeping the law. "There be some that trouble you," he wrote, "and would pervert the gospel," the good news of Christ (Galatians 1:7).

Love as a Weapon

It is a wonder that people would leave the real gospel for a counterfeit, but it is no mystery how false teachers often recruit their new disciples. Paul points out that one common technique is a zealous use of affection: "They zealously affect you, but not well; yea, they would exclude you, that ye might affect them" (Galatians 4:17).

Those who have been pulled into cults often report an incredible shower of love and attention

directed their way when the cult considered them
a hot prospect. Once a person commits to the group,
however, the zeal turns from love to indoctrination.
Rather than being overwhelmed with affection, the
new convert is put under strenuous physical discipline and eventually is worn down to the point
of exhaustion. Any feelings of self-confidence are
stripped away, leaving the person extremely suscept-
ible to the group's spiritual distortions.

The love so readily demonstrated at the beginning is only a means to isolate the individual and
bring him or her into bondage. If one doesn't go
along with the program, the love quickly ends and
the person finds himself excluded and ostracized. If
he fails to be won over to the new persuasion, the
"love" quickly turns to open hostility.

In my early years of ministry in Tucson, I had
an unpleasant encounter with a group of "Jesus
Only" Pentecostals. This cult teaches that the Father,
Son, and Holy Spirit are merely different terms for
Jesus. (Of course, they have a difficult time explain-
ing who Jesus was speaking to when He prayed to
the Father, or who it was who spoke from heaven at
Jesus' baptism. Perhaps the voice in Matthew 3:17
that said, "This is my beloved Son, in whom I am
well pleased" was just a clever bit of ventriloquism?)
The weakness of this position is evident, yet the
followers of this persuasion love to come on strong
and create all kinds of conflict.

Sadly, a couple of influential families in our
church bought into this doctrine. Soon they targeted
me as their next project and began to "zealously
affect" me. They would take me out to lunch and go
on and on about my great potential and how much
they loved the church.

Now, I have always detested arguing Scripture

with people. I usually let them lay out their faulty positions without trying to tear them apart. And so these people would quote the scripture where Jesus said, "I and my Father are one" (John 10:30) and I would say, "Yes, that is right. That is what He said." Every time they would quote Scripture I would say, "Yes, that is what it says." But I wouldn't argue with them.

Of course, I knew many scriptures that would clarify the issue, but I didn't bother to argue with these folks. Jesus said, "Agree with thine adversary quickly whiles thou art in the way with him" (Matthew 5:25), so I would agree with the scriptures they cited. While I didn't agree with their peculiar interpretations, I always agreed with the scripture itself. Since I wasn't arguing with them, these people thought they had me persuaded.

One day, they brought up their doctrine in an adult Sunday school class. When the teacher effectively refuted their position, some of them tried to claim that I was in their camp. The teacher immediately called me in to settle the dispute. When I told the class I believed that God is one yet is manifested in the distinct persons of the Father, Son, and Holy Spirit, the "Jesus Only" faction became livid.

The next day they called me on the phone and said, "We want to see you tonight at our house." That evening I visited them and they demanded, "What is the big idea, denying the truth? How could you deny what you really believe?" And I replied, "I didn't. I did not deny the truth nor did I deny what I believe. I stated in the class exactly what I believe. I don't think Jesus was playing cheap tricks of ventriloquism and I don't believe He was trying to deceive the people when He was praying to the Father. I believe that the Father, Son, and Holy Spirit are separate personalities, though there is one God." That's when I started seeing the proverbial end of the finger.

"Brother," they threatened me, "God has given us a revelation, and we had a vision of you being carried out in a black coffin unless you stand up before the church and tell them that we are right! As I listened to an avalanche of dire threats, I began to wonder, *What happened to all the love these people had for me?*

"We will give you until Saturday to make up your mind whether or not you are going to fess up," they said. I replied, "I don't need until Saturday. I can tell you right now." "Don't say another word," they answered. "Just you pray about this, brother, and if by Saturday night you won't promise that you are going to do this, then we will never be back to your church." Naturally, the leader of this group had 11 kids out of the 53 in our Sunday school. That makes it tough when you are trying to grow your Sunday school.

On Saturday night I got the call. "Well, brother, what have you decided?" "I haven't changed my mind or my thinking at all," I replied. "All right, we warned you," he said, and I heard a *click* at the other end. He was gone, and his 11 kids with him.

This man and his faction were zealous in showing affection as long as I was a potential convert. But when they discovered I wouldn't go into bondage to them and their persuasions, they dropped both me and the church like a bad habit.

That wasn't true love; it was only a hypocritical demonstration in order to make a convert out of me. As Shakespeare once observed, "Love is not love that alters, when it alteration finds." When I wasn't converted, their true feelings were displayed.

This is a frequent tactic of false teachers. They will be very zealous in their demonstration of affection in order to make a convert out of a contact. But if the person doesn't submit to their persuasions, they will quickly exclude him.

People can come on very strong and seem so loving, so nice, so sweet—but only because they are seeking to win you to their persuasion. If you are not won over, watch out! They will call you every name in the book and will hit you with all kinds of judgments and condemnations. This is not the gospel of grace!

Don't Get Tripped Up

It's always difficult to see people leave the truth for a lie. You love them and want to spare them the pain you know is ahead, but there's little you can do. Paul knew that feeling well. Galatians 5:7 is a bittersweet verse that recalls the relationship the apostle shared with the Galatians. He writes, "Ye did run well; who did hinder you that ye should not obey the truth?"

The Galatians had formerly walked in such love for God and one another that they ministered to Paul openly and selflessly in a time of extreme circumstance. They had even been willing to give up their own eyes for him. But now they had become so hindered in their walk that some considered Paul an enemy. Why? Because he cared enough to tell them the truth.

Drawing an analogy from the realm of athletics, Paul likened the Galatians to competitors who made a good start out of the blocks but then got tangled up as they ran the race. "This persuasion cometh not of him that calleth you," he wrote (Galatians 5:8). Paul

insisted that the "new and deeper truths" brought by
the Judaizers were not from God.

Each believer is responsible
to search the Scriptures to
see if the teachings are
true or false.

Yet how many people are taken in by this kind of
false persuasion? Oftentimes even sincere believers
in Christ are led astray by the clever stories of an
evangelist. They buy into false teaching not because
they have searched the Scriptures, but because
they have been influenced by the force of a persuasive personality.

The sad result of such ungodly influence is that
the victims end up in bondage, almost stripped of
their own personality. Have you ever wondered how
seemingly normal people can come so far under the
sway of a cult that they will end up selling flowers or
peanuts in the airport for their leader? This kind of
persuasion certainly doesn't come from God. In fact,
in all bondage-oriented systems, people will sooner or
later find themselves under the lordship of men.

The best safeguard against this kind of deception
is to "prove all things; hold fast that which is good"
(1 Thessalonians 5:21). No matter how highly
respected an individual is, no matter how prominent
or large a following he may have, we can't take
anyone's word for the gospel truth. Each believer is
responsible to search the Scriptures to see if these
things be so.

How tragic that we set such precaution aside and believe everything a particular teacher has to say merely because he has a certain look or speaking style or television or radio ministry. When we fail to check up on the teachings presented to us, we leave ourselves wide open to persuasions not of the one who calls us. God doesn't change His mind. God doesn't edit His truth or spice it up with new revelations. The gospel of grace doesn't change—yet it's not hard to find preachers who claim it has.

Bondage by Any Other Name

Even today there are all kinds of people who preach legalism. They will ask questions like, "How were you baptized, brother? Who baptized you? What did they say when they baptized you?" Some even say things like, "If you weren't baptized with the right formula, then it isn't a true baptism. Were you just sprinkled or were you immersed?"

The tragic thing is that these teachings serve only to alienate us from the work God has done in our hearts through faith in Jesus Christ. Any ritual, whether it is baptism or communion or foot-washing, will not avail a thing to make us righteous. Right standing with God is ours totally and completely by faith, which works by love. This is the key to real power and peace in our walk with God. No wonder the great apostle said, "I am amazed that you would so soon turn from the truth unto another gospel which isn't really a gospel"!

The true gospel *is* good news. It is the good news of God's grace and the forgiveness of sins through the finished work of Jesus Christ. Your relationship with God isn't based on your righteousness or your works or in keeping certain rules, but upon your believing in God's sacrifice for you. If you will just believe in this work of God, through Jesus Christ you can have a beautiful, unbroken relationship with God. All your sins will be washed away and the guilt of all your shortcomings, failures, and attitudes will vanish. They won't exist, for you will have been justified through faith in Jesus Christ.

Paul knew the folly of trying to relate to God on the basis of works. He could see the end result, for that's where he started out. "Don't tell me about the law," he might say, "I know all about the law. I know all about the righteousness which was of the law. I was a Pharisee. I was zealous. I was more zealous than my brothers. Don't give me that business of the law; I know what it is all about. But thank God, I was delivered from all that when I came into a new relationship with God through faith in Jesus Christ!"

We have been, too. Therefore, having been established in the gospel of grace, don't let men trouble you and lay guilt trips or the idea of righteousness by works upon you. It's not worth it. None of us need a word like *anathema* to be attached to our name.

12

Grace

All or Nothing

S OME TIME AGO I attended a pastor's luncheon in Oregon. Before the program began, someone asked if I had heard about the hitchhiker who spoke about the Lord's return and then vanished. I told him yes, I had. Only the first time I had heard about it was way back in 1944 in Burbank, California. The story always had the same ending. The couple who picked up the hitchhiker pull into a service station only to hear the attendant tell them they are the ninth customers that day with the same story. The pastor who questioned me laughed and said, "That shows you how remote Oregon is—it took 50 years for this rumor to get here!"

How prone we are to getting all worked up over things that amount to nothing! And how grateful I am that our faith is based on the firm foundation

of the Word of God. I would much prefer that the
Lord speak to me from the tried and true pages of
Scripture than to receive some kind of supernatural,
special revelation. If even an angel came to me claim-
ing to have some revolutionary truth, I would find
myself questioning whether his message was of
God.

Endless second-guessing is not a problem when
we turn to the Word. The Bible is the only firm foundation for our faith and Christian walk. When our
lives are founded on the truth of God's Word, we won't
be carried away by the latest doctrinal fad or "new
and improved" version of the gospel. How crucial it
is that we stand fast on the truth of God's Word! This
is the only way to maintain the glorious liberty provided to us so abundantly in Christ.

How Can We Stand Fast?

It is important to understand that those who fail
to stand fast are moved from simple faith in Christ by
a lack of understanding of God's Word. It is only a
solid grasp of the Scriptures that brings real stability
to our lives.

Paul once observed that God has provided the
church with apostles, prophets, evangelists, and
pastor-teachers for the "perfecting of the saints"
(Ephesians 4:11,12). A mark of this perfection is a
unity of faith so stable that we will be "no more children, tossed to and fro, and carried about with every
wind of doctrine, by the sleight of men, and cunning
craftiness, whereby they lie in wait to deceive"
(Ephesians 4:14). How important it is for us to be
founded on the Word, especially in our deception-
ridden times!

From the materialistic excesses of the prosperity

movement ("Of course God wants all His children to drive Mercedes. You only drive a Toyota? How unspiritual can you be?") to "new" revelations about the only proper way to be baptized, strange twists of doctrine are the rule nowadays, not the exception.

When Paul exhorts his friends in Galatians 5:1 to "stand fast therefore in the liberty wherewith Christ hath made us free, and be not entangled again with the yoke of bondage," his message is as relevant for us today as when he first wrote his letter. Oftentimes the church itself will be the first to impose a legalistic standard of righteousness upon us. These rules and regulations are usually well-received because there is a certain security to the well-defined limitations a law provides. The cults offer people an overwhelming degree of personal direction and the "security" that comes from blind obedience to authority.

But those who give themselves to such strictly regimented lifestyles do so at the cost of personal freedom. They fail to realize that along with the sense of security these groups provide comes an intense level of condemnation if one breaks from the standards. Many who were enslaved in such systems tell us they believed that leaving the group was tantamount to leaving God. If a convert begins to question the group or wants to go somewhere else, they are told they are in danger of hell. These kind of pressure tactics and outrageous claims to an exclusive lock on the truth are the earmarks of bondage-based groups.

On the other hand, a church that encourages people to find a place where they will be able to grow in their walk with the Lord shows a sign of spiritual health. At Calvary Chapel, we often suggest that people look around and find a place that can minister most effectively to them. Some who come to our fellowship would like to see more emotionalism or sensationalism in our services. We encourage these people to exercise their freedom by finding a place more in keeping with their desires. We are not interested in seeing anyone bound to our church.

It is vital for us to embrace this truth: Putting our faith in any work cuts us off from the grace of God.

Paul's use of the phrase "yoke of bondage" is probably a reference to the words of Simon Peter at the first Jerusalem Council. In Acts 15, Peter recounted God's call for him to minister to the Gentiles at the house of Cornelius. He suggested that the council not place upon non-Jews a yoke of bondage "which neither our fathers nor we were able to bear" (verse 10). Paul cites Peter's words to emphasize that the message of freedom in grace was not something he developed on his own. This liberty in Christ was the solid position of the church.

Rituals Do Not Save

A key aspect of the teaching rejected at the Jerusalem Council was the insistence that Gentiles go through the ritual of circumcision in order to be saved. The council agreed with Paul that works cannot possibly make anyone righteous. Paul later stated that putting faith in a ritual runs counter to the gospel. He wrote, "Behold, I Paul say unto you, that if ye

be circumcised, Christ shall profit you nothing"
(Galatians 5:2).

This permits us to safely say that putting our
faith in *any* work cuts us off from the grace of God.
It is vital for us to embrace this truth. Not many
teachers go around anymore advocating circumcision
for salvation, but how many times have we heard
very sincere people insist that we must go through
the ritual of baptism in order to be saved?

Some take this principle to all kinds of strange
extremes. There are sects who teach that not only
must we be baptized to be saved, but we also must
be baptized "correctly." Some insist we must be
baptized in the name of Jesus only. Others maintain
it must be done by an ordained minister of their particular denomination. Some get so obsessed with
technicalities that they have split churches over sprin-
kling or immersion, or even whether people should
be baptized forward or backward!

The root of all this division is an improper trust
in a particular good work to achieve right standing
with God. The clear teaching of Scripture is that if we
trust in *any* good work for salvation, then Christ is
of no value to us. We can't ride both sides of the
fence and trust Christ and our good works. If we
trust in baptism as the basis of our salvation, we
are putting our faith in works. We are building our
spiritual house on a sandy foundation that will be
incapable of sustaining us.

A few years ago, a young man came to me and
told me he was no longer a Christian, but had joined
the Mormon church. When I asked in what he was
trusting as his hope for eternal life, he replied his
hope was based on his faith in Jesus Christ *and* continued membership in the Mormon church. I frankly
told him his decision was tragic. The moment he put

his trust in anything other than the finished work of Jesus Christ alone, he had gone too far.

All we need to stand righteously before God is faith in Christ. If we insist on trusting in Jesus *and* circumcision (or baptism or tithing or continued membership in a church), then Christ will be of no value to us whatsoever.

It's *All* or *Nothing*

Those who depend on their works for righteousness can't adopt a pick-and-choose approach. If we accept one good work as necessary for salvation, we become debtors to the whole law; we must keep the law in its entirety. As Paul pointed out in Galatians 3:10, "For as many as are of the works of the law are under the curse: for it is written, Cursed is every one that continueth not in all things which are written in the book of the law to do them." James amplified this truth when he stated, "Whosoever shall keep the whole law, and yet offend in one point, he is guilty of all" (James 2:10).

If we look to the law for righteousness, not only will Christ avail us nothing, but we also will have to keep every command to utter perfection. Our relationship with God is predicated on legalism or grace.

Paul pulled no punches in his rejection of the false teaching of the Judaizers. He wrote, "Christ is become of no effect unto you, whosoever of you are justified by the law; ye are fallen from grace" (Galatians 5:4). Those who bring their holier-than-thou sounding package to Christianity have rejected grace.

It is helpful to remember that no one will be in heaven because of his good works. We will not have to listen to Abraham or David or Paul talk about all the wonderful things they did to achieve a righteous standing before God. These men simply believed

God, and their faith was accounted for righteousness. None of us will stand in heaven comparing good works with one another because there will be only one whose works will be honored before the throne of God—our Lord, Jesus Christ. Jesus and Jesus alone will receive the glory for our salvation. If it were not for Him, none of us would get there.

As Paul put it, "God forbid that I should glory, save in the cross of Jesus Christ" (Galatians 6:14). No matter how many good deeds we've done for Him, no matter how many people we lead to Him or churches we establish for Him, our only glory is in Jesus Christ, who died for us. Our righteousness is not a question of good works, human efforts, keeping certain rituals or dietary laws. Our righteousness both at this moment and for all eternity is a result of our simple faith in God's Son, Jesus.

Righteousness by faith removes all the distinctions between those who belong to Christ. I am no better than you, or you than me. We are all sinners, saved only by God's glorious grace. There is no other way to right standing before God. There is only one kind of righteousness that God will accept: the imputed righteousness of Jesus Christ.

This is no small side issue for us as believers. We must stand fast in the liberty wherein Christ has made us free. We must not allow condemning rules to come in and dominate our lives until we feel that, unless we are praying seven hours a day or reading 25 chapters of Scripture in our devotions, we are not really righteous. Our righteousness is not predicated upon how much we read, pray, fast, or give. Our righteousness is based upon simple trust in Jesus to wash us and cleanse us of our sins and to make us pure in the eyes of the Father.

The work of our salvation has been done. There is nothing we can do to improve it. Our good works result from God's acceptance and love; we don't do works to earn His love. Walking according to Christ's commands doesn't make us more righteous— just happier and more satisfied. What better way to live than giving my existence to the one who loves me so much in the here and now and who has promised to take care of me forever? To be led and guided by God is the most fulfilling experience in the world.

Two Choices Only

All of us are either trying to work and be good enough to please God, or we are believing and trusting God to do for us what we can't do for ourselves. At each moment of our lives we find ourselves on one road or the other. If we are still trying to please God through being good enough, defeat and frustration will be our lot. If we have trusted in God's grace to transform us and form Christ within us, we will enjoy life and peace.

I learned the timeless lesson that laws and rule-keeping can never change our hearts.

I recall one incident when our family misguidedly tried to make a concerted effort at bringing a more Christlike atmosphere to our home. As our children were growing up there came a time when sibling rivalry seemed to be at an all-time high. Somehow our children had gotten into the habit of calling each other names. We found that addressing each other as "dummy," "stupid," or "idiot" had a way of creating friction. So we tried to bring some discipline to the situation and set up some rules.

Now, in a two-story house, one of the most distasteful tasks is vacuuming the stairs. So in order to improve the tenor of our home life, we decided to keep records of family members who insulted each other. The one with the most violations had to vacuum the stairs. All this seemed very reasonable at the time, but to this day, I have the sneaky feeling that I was being set up.

One day our two boys started to get into some mischief. When I came into the room they were in the middle of destroying, the first words out of my mouth were, "What stupid idiot left this mess?" No doubt you can figure out who ended up vacuuming the stairs.

One good thing came out of it, however. I learned again the timeless lesson that laws and rule-keeping can never change our hearts. Our motives were good. We all struggled in this family endeavor at righteousness—yet we all fell miserably short.

It seems that no matter how hard we try to be holy, we have to face the fact that our righteousness is as filthy rags in the sight of the Lord. God has provided a different hope of righteousness for us—a standing and a relationship with Himself that we must receive as a gift. Righteousness is imparted to us by believing in Jesus Christ and knowing that we can't live up to a perfect standard. This is the crucial choice set before us. We can try to clean up our old, tattered, dirty rags and try to look presentable in heaven; or we can choose to be robed in the complete righteousness of Christ by faith.

My vacuum cleaner reminds me that my only hope is to choose grace.

Off Course and Out of Sight

It never ceases to amaze me how easy it is to get off course in the Christian life. Even a seemingly minor flaw in a relatively small area of faith or practice can get us completely off center in almost every facet of our Christian life. Therefore, making every effort to maintain doctrinal purity is growing more important every day.

Recently I had the opportunity to discuss spiritual issues with a fellow who believed the church would go through the Great Tribulation. He wondered why I would take such a strong stand on what he considered an unimportant facet of eschatology. I responded by asking, "If the church is going to go through the Great Tribulation, who are the 144,000 mentioned in the book of Revelation?" He replied that these people were part of the church because the church is spiritual Israel. I then asked him if he believed that all of God's promises to national Israel were somehow spiritually fulfilled in the church. He agreed that they were. "How interesting," I said, "that such an 'unimportant' area of eschatology has completely affected your doctrine of the church as well." To put it in Paul's terms, "a little leaven leaveneth the whole lump" (Galatians 5:9).

Let's put it another way. Imagine you are traveling by plane from Los Angeles to Hawaii. Before takeoff, the pilot comes on the loudspeaker and says, "Well folks, we're having a slight problem with our navigational system, but don't worry about it. We'll not be more than two degrees off course." Two degrees wouldn't be much just out of Los Angeles, but by the time we were 3,000 miles over the Pacific, we would be hopelessly lost. The Big Island would be nowhere in sight.

Clearly, the best approach is to avoid being even a slight degree off course. In matters of doctrine, it is imperative that we search the Scriptures, prove all things, and avoid being taken in by the persuasive arguments of men. That is how we stand in grace.

Costly Vigilance

Don't be deceived—this vigilance costs something. Controversy and persecution have surrounded the preaching of the gospel from the beginning. As Paul remarked in Galatians 5:11, "And I, brethren, if I yet preach circumcision, why do I yet suffer persecution? Then is the offense of the cross ceased." If Paul were preaching that a right standing with God could be gained by a series of good works, there would be no opposition to Christianity. But the cross of Christ has always been an offense.

The cross shows us there is only one way to be righteous before God. The true message of salvation in Christ alone offends people because it is so narrow and exclusive. The cross declares to the world that there is only one hope for eternal life, the death and resurrection of Jesus Christ. Paul is in essence saying, "If I want to be liberal and say, 'Circumcision is fine if it works for you,' then no one would persecute me. But I am being persecuted because I have cared enough to stand for the truth."

Paul was never one to mince words. We can see his emotional commitment to the truth in his verbal broadside against those consumed with the issue of circumcision. "I would they were even cut off which trouble you," he wrote in Galatians 5:12. The term rendered "cut off" in the King James Version literally means "to emasculate" or "castrate." Paul meant, "If these false teachers believe a little mutilation of the flesh makes us righteous, then why don't they go all the way and start with themselves while they're at it!" A modern parallel to Paul's statement might be, "I wish those who tell you righteousness comes through baptism would go all the way and drown themselves!" Paul vented his feelings toward those who would dare to pervert the glorious gospel of grace.

Think of how heartsick these developments must have made the apostle. Here was a fellowship where the Spirit was working, where people were in love with God and each other. There was unity and excitement in the Lord until these false teachers arrived on the scene. With the introduction of their own version of the gospel, they created division and soon factions began to develop. The beautiful love and fellowship this body had known soon became but a distant memory. No wonder Paul's denunciation of their teaching was so direct!

Thanks, Paul!

We who have come to the glorious saving grace of Jesus Christ owe Paul a great measure of thanks. If it were not for him, many in the church might easily have become part of just another Jewish sect. But it was Paul who stood firm and established new believers in the grace of Jesus Christ. His stand cost him something. He was persecuted and slandered and viciously opposed for most of his ministry. But it was worth it. At the end of his life he could write these stirring words, "I have fought a good fight, I have finished my course, I have kept the faith: Henceforth there is laid up for me a crown of righteousness, which the Lord, the righteous judge, shall give me at that day: and not to me only, but unto all them also that love his appearing" (2 Timothy 4:7,8).

May God give us the grace to stand for the truth and the wisdom to share it in love. May He grant that we stand fast in Jesus Christ and in the knowledge of the truth. May we realize the incredible depth of blessing and freedom that God has so richly granted to us. And may we experience these blessings daily as we walk in God's beautiful love, standing fast in His glorious grace.

13
Grace
Members of
Royalty

AS A CHILD, did you ever wonder what it would be like to be born into royalty? Those of us who came from poorer backgrounds probably spent quite a bit of time daydreaming of what it would be like to be rich.

We may not come from wealthy families, but the Bible makes it clear that because of our relationship with Christ, we are made into a spiritual nation of descendants through faith. As Paul writes in Galatians 3:29, "if ye be Christ's, then are ye Abraham's seed, and heirs according to the promise." When we trace our true heritage, we find our identity no longer rooted in Europe or Asia or Africa. By grace we can trace our true lineage back to Christ, the fulfillment of God's promise to Abraham. And because of this

special relationship, we are now heirs of the very
kingdom of God.

What Is an Heir?

A child of six or seven who receives a large
inheritance is, technically speaking, a very wealthy
person. Yet until this child reaches the age of majority, as stipulated in the will left by his parents, he is
no different in practical position than a hired servant
in the home. Certainly all the physical needs of the
heir will be met, but he will have no authority to
decide how his inheritance will be handled until he
comes of age.

The life situation of an heir has not changed con-
siderably since the time of Paul. Paul wrote, "Now I
say, that the heir, as long as he is a child, differeth
nothing from a servant, though he be lord of all; But
is under tutors and governors until the time appointed
of the father" (Galatians 4:1,2). Paul explains that the
heir found himself under the authority of a steward
who had been given full responsibility to manage the
estate. Typically, a guardian also would be appointed
to oversee the child's upbringing and to teach him
right and wrong until he grew to adulthood.

In Roman society, a boy was considered an infant
until he was seven years old. From this time until
age 17, a small, purple band would encircle his robe,
identifying him as a child. At age 17 he would be
given another robe without the purple band to indi-
cate he should be considered a man. Still, not until he
reached the age of 25 did he enjoy the legal right to
get involved in business affairs.

Things were somewhat simpler in Jewish culture. At age 12, a boy would go through a ceremony
known as a bar mitzvah, in which he would become a

full-fledged "son of the covenant." The father of the boy would stand and offer a prayer of thanks that he was no longer responsible for his son's actions. The boy in turn would offer a prayer accepting personal responsibility for himself as a man.

Paul uses this well-known transition to adulthood to illustrate the relationship of the law to God's people. When Israel was placed under the law, it was made heir of the promises of God. Yet as long as the nation was under the law, the promises of their glorious inheritance would not be fulfilled. They awaited the day called "the fulness of the time" when God would make good on His every promise through the provision of His Son. Until that time, Israel was much like a small child under the governing control of the law.

The Bondage of the Law

The law covered nearly every contingency of day-to-day life, from diet to business transactions to marital relationships. The law exercised strict oversight over God's people until the time they would "graduate" from childhood to adulthood, when at last they could enjoy the full benefits of the inheritance promised to them. The promise of a new and wonderful relationship with God through the coming of the Messiah had been given to Israel, and yet this promise could not be fulfilled until the time appointed by the Father.

The law provided a framework for both individuals and even an entire society to live in order and harmony. If such external guidelines are all we have in our relationship with God, however, we find ourselves in a form of bondage. That is why Paul wrote, "Even so we, when we were children, were in bondage under the elements of the world" (Galatians 4:3).

---

*The law can never take
us into the rich, full,
free life that the
Holy Spirit wants for us.*

When Paul refers to the "elements of the world," he is speaking of what we would call the basics of life. The law of Moses was quite effective concerning these kinds of foundational "do's and don'ts" of daily living.

I have always found it ironic that the first church council (described in Acts 15) dealt so strongly with the question of a complex code of behavior governing the life of believers. Even though they concluded that believers were no longer obligated to slavishly follow a code of external behavior, there are still many churches today that seek to impose similar control over their people.

I grew up in a church that believed it had a divine mandate to tell women how they should dress and what was appropriate or inappropriate in hairstyles. The leaders also seemed to believe they had a revelation about God's opinions on makeup. As children, we were given endless commands about what we could or could not do. I wouldn't go so far as to say the church put us back under the law of Moses, but it did lay such a heavy load of condemnation and bondage on me that I wasn't able to bear up under its weight. I was constantly repenting because I simply couldn't live up to the standards they had set up.

The law could never take us into the rich, full, free life that the Holy Spirit wants for us. It only brings guilt, condemnation, and frustration. Fortunately, the law is not the end of the story.

When the Time Came

In Paul's day, the legal procedures governing the granting of an inheritance were very precise. When a child reached the age specified in a will for majority, there was no longer a need for a guardian or a steward to exercise oversight. The heir could receive what was promised directly when he came of age in "the fulness of the time."

Paul had that in mind when he wrote, "When the fulness of the time was come, God sent forth his Son, made of a woman, made under the law" (Galatians 4:4). Since Jesus has come, we can experience the fullness of blessing God has promised. But there is another shade of meaning to this notion of "the fulness of the time." Have you ever wondered why God allowed his people to live under the law for nearly 1,400 years before He sent His Son? To be honest, we may never fully understand God's timing. His ways are not our ways, and His thoughts are not our thoughts. But if we take a brief look at history, we may see many obvious reasons why the timing of Jesus' arrival on the human scene was especially opportune.

First, Christ was born in an era of unprecedented peace. For over 13 years before the birth of Christ and throughout His lifetime, the gates to the temple of Janus in Rome were closed. Whenever Rome went to war, this temple would be crowded with worshipers praying to Janus for victory. But in Christ's era, the classic Pax Romana was firmly in place.

Rome also had made huge strides forward in transportation, creating a well-designed system of roads stretching across the empire. And Greek, a clear, expressive, and remarkably specific language, had become the universal tongue under Roman rule.

All these factors contributed to the rapid spread of the gospel in the first century. It may well be that God waited for this strategic moment so that the message of His love and forgiveness for all mankind might enjoy a worldwide impact.

Notice as well that Paul spoke of Christ being "sent" by the Father, implying not only the eternal preexistence of Christ, but also that Jesus came with a specific purpose in mind. Jesus was sent into this world to complete the redemption of humanity. He came to establish a new covenant whereby man could relate to God in intimacy and enter into the fullness of His promised blessings.

Paul also tells us that Jesus was "made of a woman, made under the law." This reference to the virgin birth strongly alludes to the first promise of the Messiah given in Scripture. In Genesis 3:15, God promised that the seed of the woman would bruise the head of the serpent, destroying the works of death and separation from God that Satan had brought about in the Garden of Eden. Jesus also was "made under the law," a reminder that Christ was born a Jew and was sent first to redeem the Jewish people. He came that the people of God might finally achieve spiritual adulthood and enjoy the whole of their spiritual inheritance. Only through Jesus would they receive their inheritance from the heavenly Father.

What a Dad!

I often miss a dear, departed saint by the name of Iva Newman who was involved at Calvary from the beginning. This godly woman walked with God more years than I have lived. I used to love to hear her pray. "Now, Father dear . . ." she would say. Oh, how I loved that! She enjoyed a close, beautiful, intimate fellowship with God. She related to God as her "Father dear."

Did you know that the death and resurrection of Christ has won for you that same kind of rich, close relationship? That was Paul's point when he wrote, "Because ye are sons, God hath sent forth the Spirit of his Son into your hearts, crying Abba, Father" (Galatians 4:6).

In this passage we see a marvelous picture of the involvement of the entire Trinity in the life of the believer: God the Father sends forth the Spirit of His Son into our hearts. A parallel passage found in Romans 8:15,16 tells us that the Spirit of God Himself bears witness with our spirit that we are the sons of God. This kind of relationship is possible only if we experience a complete spiritual rebirth. As Jesus Himself put it, "That which is born of the flesh is flesh; and that which is born of the Spirit is spirit. Marvel not that I said unto thee, Ye must be born again" (John 3:6,7). When we are born again spiritually, we are given the power to enter into a wonderfully intimate relationship with God, typified by Paul's use of the term "Abba."

Abba is an endearing term for "father." It's an Aramaic word; and if you visit Israel even today you'll constantly hear the little children calling out, "Abba! Abba!" They're saying, "Daddy! Daddy!"

Jesus often used the term. No doubt His disciples heard Him use it so frequently in His prayer life that they did not translate the word into Greek. They preserved the Aramaic expression because they wanted to capture the same warmth and intimacy Jesus shared with His Father.

> *It is God's intent that*
> *we come to know Him as*
> *our loving Father,*
> *even as our Dad.*

How wonderful it is to know that God wants the same loving, personal relationship with us in our walk with Him! Too often we are prone to see God as a great, distant, all-powerful Creator, but it is God's intent that we come to know Him as our loving Father, even as our Dad.

Some see this kind of familiarity as disrespectful, yet it is God Himself who calls us to such a level of intimacy. I recall a time when I had the opportunity to meet with a group of Italian believers for a prayer meeting. For my benefit they were praying in English, but even then they kept referring to God as "Papa." At first I thought this was getting just a tad too informal; but a moment's reflection made me reconsider. There was a depth of love and closeness in that expression that rang true to Scripture.

How remarkable it is that God now welcomes us into His presence as dearly loved children and not fearful, cringing slaves. Isn't this the way a relationship between a father and his children should be? When my children come to visit they don't stand at attention, salute, and quiver in fear as they talk with me. They don't approach me with all kinds of pretentious formality and say, "Oh, exalted father, grant this humble request of your child this day." Usually it's more like, "Hey Dad, I need five bucks. I don't have time to explain; just give it to me now and I'll fill you in later!"

God desires that our time with Him be relaxing and restoring to our hearts. He wants us to feel at home with Him and to be free and open in our relationship. We might as well feel that way since our lives are an open book before Him anyway. He knows us better than we know ourselves.

God doesn't want us to have a cold, aloof, arms-length relationship with Him. God wants us to know His love personally in the very depths of our heart. Whatever expression that communicates such closeness is completely acceptable, whether that is "Father," "Dad," or even "Papa."

The Ideal Dad

God is our Father in the purest, truest, most holy sense. He is our Father in an ideal way. God help us, our corrupted culture has destroyed the father image in the hearts of many children. That's tragic. I thank God for my godly father, who always has helped me relate to God in a very close, glorious way. I feel sorry for people who can't relate to the fatherhood of God in their lives because of some corrupted example.

Whatever your experience has been, God wants you to relate to Him in that closest kind of fellowship, that intimacy, and to know him as a loving, righteous Father, a holy and pure and caring Father. His Spirit within our hearts cries out, "Abba! Daddy! Father!"

God is able to bestow upon us His love, lavishing us with His kindness and His goodness, that we might come to love Him more and more. This is the purpose of God for man. Your life will never be complete until the purposes of God have been accomplished in you—until you relate to God in that close, personal way, until you say, "Oh, Abba!" and feel it from your heart.

Dads, do you remember the first time your child said, "Daddy"? It's very distinguishable. You understood it completely. My own little girl was so smart. The first word she said was, "Daddy." That's right—clear as can be. I turned, I screamed, I shouted, "What?" I was sad that nobody else was around, because who would believe me? I tried to get her to say it again and she gave me the sweetest, most knowing smile—but she wouldn't repeat it. Still, I heard it! Soon she was saying it in front of everybody and I was so thrilled.

On that day when we first say, "Oh, Abba!" and He hears us, God is thrilled. It's the beginning of a relationship where from the heart we can say, "Hey, that's my Abba. That's my Daddy." The wonder is that this is just the beginning of the richness of our fellowship with God.

Heirs of God

As incomprehensibly great as it is to enter into a relationship with God as our "Abba," that is not the end of the story. Paul tells us, "Wherefore thou art no more a servant, but a son; and if a son, then an heir of God" (Galatians 4:7). By coming into this relationship with God as His adopted sons, His Spirit now in our hearts crying, "Oh, Abba," we have become heirs of God. We are heirs of God's eternal, glorious kingdom.

Our Father loves us so much he has generously made us His heirs, and this spiritual inheritance is intended by God to be a very real and present blessing in our lives.

Some make the mistake of thinking that a believer has to wait until heaven to enjoy his inheritance, but nothing could be further from the truth. The Bible tells us that the earmarks of the kingdom of God are righteousness, peace, and joy in the Holy Spirit (Romans 14:17). We can cash in on these wonderful blessings in the here and now. The peace of God which passes all understanding can keep our hearts and minds *right now*. Our soul can overflow with joy unspeakable and full of glory *right now*. We can experience a liberating freedom from guilt and fear because we have been declared completely righteous by our believing in the finished work of Jesus Christ.

That's Not All, Folks!

These are just a few of the elements of our glorious inheritance that already are ours because God has made us joint heirs with Jesus. We can enter into the place of highest blessing because of the wonderful love and grace of our heavenly "Dad."

And yet, that is not all. Jesus said there is coming a day when He will say to those on His right hand, "Come, ye blessed of my Father, inherit the kingdom prepared for you from the foundation of the world" (Matthew 25:34). I'm an heir of God; I'm the adopted son of the King. So if my Father is the King of the universe, that must make me Prince Charles!

It also makes you a prince or a princess. It makes you an heir of the kingdom—the kingdom that God wants you to share with Him and to enjoy, world without end. And then will the purposes of God for man be accomplished, when man is restored into this full, complete, intimate fellowship with God.

Our hearts can overflow with thanksgiving for the warmth and security we now feel in knowing of

God's limitless love and concern for us. What strength there is in the sure knowledge that He will take care of us, watch over us, and keep us in His love. We can live with confidence and be sure that we have a Father who is for us, solidly behind us every step of the way, granting us tremendous resources that we might walk with Him in newness of life.

Our "Abba" is committed to keeping us from falling and to present us faultless before His presence with exceeding joy (*see* Jude 24). He has granted us sonship and an incorruptible inheritance through Jesus Christ our Lord. Not because we deserve it. Not because we've earned it. All of this has been made possible only through His rich mercy and grace.

How wonderful it is that when we are born again we discover that, in a unique way, we have become both spiritually wealthy and members of royalty in the best and truest sense of the term. Because we are children of God, we have been made princes and princesses of the kingdom. Because of what Christ has done for us, we will receive an inheritance that is incorruptible and undefiled and will not fade away— and it is waiting for every one of us to enjoy for all eternity.

14
Grace

Our Sole
Responsibility

THE MESSAGE OF THE New Testament is simple, direct, and unmistakable. We are saved by God's grace through faith alone, not on the basis of any good works we have done. The sole responsibility of a Christian is to believe in the love and grace which God freely offers.

This clear message stands in sharp contrast to the teachings of those who want us to trust in Christ *and* obey certain rules or practice certain rites. These teachers call their message a gospel, but it isn't really good news at all. They claim that in order to be acceptable to God, we need to do adequate works. Law and works are placed side by side with grace as a two-part ticket to righteousness. Contrary to these teachers, however, the New Testament insists that it is not law and works that justify, but God's grace and our response of faith.

We are faced with a classic either/or situation. Righteousness must either come by faith in Christ alone, or by a perfect keeping of God's law. Right standing with God by faith or salvation by works are mutually exclusive. When we seek righteousness before God, we must make our choice and not look for some compromising middle ground.

Abraham was a man who simply believed God, and God accounted him righteous. We stand on the same ground as Abraham and are heirs of the same blessings and promises that he enjoyed. This place of privilege comes only by faith, not by obedience to a code of law or a set of rules. If we seek to be righteous before God by our works, rather than by faith, we find ourselves under a curse. There are no exceptions to this rule.

If we look to the law as our hope of assurance before God, the only way we can know security is to keep every commandment flawlessly. As Paul wrote, "Cursed is every one that continueth not in all things which are written in the book of the law to do them" (Galatians 3:10). This means we could never really know if we were saved until we died, and who can live with that kind of pressure?

Imagine that you lived a perfect life, keeping every commandment, never committing a wrong action. One day, you decide to cross the street while the walk sign is lit. Suddenly, some driver runs the red light and strikes you down. As you watch his car's transmission pass over your head, you raise your fist and your parting words before leaving this world are your assessment of this idiot's driving habits. In that one small act, you missed the mark. You fell from perfection. You sinned—and the Bible says the wages of sin is death.

You may be able to keep nine of God's commandments perfectly, but if you fall short on number ten, you've missed the target. You have sinned. And the bad news is, unless you keep the whole law and do all that is written in it, you are guilty. It doesn't matter which law you violate; just one failure puts you out.

Therefore, you don't stand a ghost of a chance of being declared righteous on the basis of your goodness. You are already out. You've already missed the mark. All you can expect is the curse of the law. Justification by good works is impossible because it relies on imperfect human effort. Legalism is the way of the curse.

Conversely, the avenue of true righteousness and blessing is the way of faith because it relies not on your effort but on God's great mercy and abundant grace toward you in Jesus Christ. Though you have missed the mark—though you have utterly failed to be righteous by your own efforts—God has justified you in His Son. Jesus took the responsibility for your falling short of God's standard and paid the penalty that you owed but could never pay. He gives you His perfect righteousness if you will just believe in Him and place your faith in Him. And now, being made right with God through Him, you are a beneficiary of all the wonderful blessings of God.

A Tragic Error

One of the most tragic errors the church can make is to emphasize the work that believers should be doing for God. How many times have you heard heavy, condemning sermons that tell you, "You ought to be praying more! You ought to be giving more!

You ought to be witnessing more, or reading your Bible more, or serving God on some committee more!" How often do you go to church looking for encouragement only to hear about your failure and how disappointed God must be with you?

The last thing I need is for someone to lay a heavy burden on me about my failures. I know I ought to be doing more. No one needs to tell me that I don't pray enough or read my Bible enough or give to God enough. All I get from such messages is a huge guilt complex. My frustration increases because I really *want* to love God more, to pray more, to have a deeper fellowship with Him. When we place our emphasis on areas of failure, we end up creating defeated, discouraged Christians who give up and drop out of the race.

What a different message we see when we turn to the New Testament! It highlights not what we ought to be doing for God, but what God has already done for us. What we can do for God can never be enough. Our efforts at righteousness are always marred by our imperfections. But what God has done for us is perfect, beautiful, complete, and fantastic. How sad that we have reversed the equation and constantly harp upon our responsibility instead of God's wonderful grace! This is why we see so much of the church on the verge of dying out. We don't need someone to remind us of our failure as much as we need someone to show us the way out of our predicament. We need grace, not guilt.

Your One Duty

God has given you but one simple responsibility: to believe in His promise. You can enjoy the blessing of a relationship with God even though you may not pray enough, or give enough, or sacrifice enough because of your faith in what God has already done for you.

God made Jesus to be sin for you that you might be made the righteousness of God through Him. Jesus imparts to you His righteousness when you simply place your faith and trust in the work He has done for you. His work is all of grace.

Paul opened his letter to the Galatians with the salutation, "Grace be to you." He closed it with, "Brethren, the grace of our Lord Jesus Christ be with your spirit. Amen." His benediction takes on a rich depth of meaning in light of the letter's sharp focus on the glorious grace of God. The grace of Jesus, not the law of Moses, was the Galatians' greatest need. To walk in the power of His Spirit, not in the vain efforts of the flesh, was their calling.

How did the Galatians respond? We are not told. Perhaps this is because the question raised in Galatia is always an open one. Will you rely on your own righteousness, or will you trust in God's gracious provision? Will you remain in the simple message of salvation by grace through faith? Or will you add your own list of righteous works to the finished work of Christ? Will you walk in the flesh or in the Spirit? Will you glory in the cross of Christ alone? Or will you seek the approval and rewards of this world so that you may glory in your flesh?

These are issues that every believer in every generation eventually must wrestle with. The answers you stand for will spell the difference between peace and fear, pride and true humility, even spiritual life and death.

May you stand without wavering for the grace of Jesus Christ. May you not be moved by the deceptive desire to please men. May you be so heavenly minded that you are of the greatest earthly good, holding out the word of life in an increasingly dark and hopeless world. And may you glory this day in what Jesus has done for you, and in that alone.

Discover Intimacy with God
in these Harvest House Books

EVERY DAY WITH JESUS
by *Greg Laurie*

Every Day with Jesus invites you to take an intimate walk with the Savior, following His path from heaven's glory to a stable, from a cruel death to a magnificent resurrection. Along the way, hear the Master's own words about how to live a life that pleases God. Catch fresh glimpses of how He longs to use us to draw other people into the loving arms of the Father. These brief, powerful meditations, rooted in God's Word and sprinkled with good humor, will carry you on a surprising and life-changing journey with the King of kings and Lord of lords.

THE GRACE EXCHANGE
by *Larry Huntsperger*

Many people struggle to know victory and joy, but instead experience disappointment and frustration. They long to know that they are fully loved and accepted by God, but misguided thoughts such as "Godly people don't have ungodly desires"; "I will be accepted by God when I...."; and "If I just try harder, I will succeed" steal their confidence. The secret to freedom is found in the way we *think* about the Christian life. In *The Grace Exchange*, you'll discover the heart of victorious Christian living and learn how to experience the spiritual fulfillment you long for!

IN HIS PRESENCE
by *Ray and Anne Ortlund*

In this masterful book on the adventure of knowing Christ, the Ortlunds share joyous, life-changing truths about God's forgiveness, His cleansing, and His ever-present love. The simplicity in Christian maturity comes from knowing that God is awesome yet approachable, almighty yet intimate, majestic yet merciful. In short devotional chapters, Ray and Anne open our eyes to God's daily presence and remind us that He has been there forever—loving us, making plans for us, caring for us. *In His Presence* encourages us to slip into God's presence quietly, humbly, and begin to discover His thoughts and plans for us.